ROGER TORY PETERSON

THE ART AND PHOTOGRAPHY OF THE WORLD'S FOREMOST BIRDER

ROGER TORY PETERSON

THE ART AND PHOTOGRAPHY OF THE WORLD'S FOREMOST BIRDER

EDITED BY
Roger Tory Peterson and
Rudy Hoglund

FOREWORD BY
S. Dillon Ripley

WATCHING THE BIRDS BY
William Zinsser

COMMENTARIES BY
John Leo

Previous pages: Penguins, seen in this oil on canvas painting executed for the book *The World of Birds,* are Peterson's favorite family of birds. He is nick-named "King Penguin" by some of his friends, and he has made seventeen trips to the Antarctic. Clockwise (from the large penguin): King, Little Blue, Chinstrap, Rockhopper, Adélie, Gentoo, Royal, Galápagos, and Humboldt penguins.

Editor: Charles Miers
Designer: Rudy Hoglund
Compositor: Rose Scarpetis

First published in the United States of America in 1994 by
Rizzoli International Publications, Inc.
300 Park Avenue South, New York, New York 10010

Library of Congress Cataloging-in-Publication Data

Peterson, Roger Tory, 1908–
    Roger Tory Peterson : art and photography of the world's
foremost birder / edited by Roger Tory Peterson and Rudy Hoglund :
foreword by S. Dillon Ripley ; commentaries by John Leo.
        p.   cm.
    ISBN 0-8478-1816-0
    1. Peterson, Roger Tory, 1908–   . 2. Ornithologists—United
States—Biography. 3. Birds—Pictorial Works. I. Hoglund, Rudy.
II. Title.
QL31.P45A3   1994
598'.092—dc20
[B]   94-14288
                                                             CIP

Printed and bound in Japan

ACKNOWLEDGMENTS

OVER THE LAST FIFTY YEARS, THE POPULARITY OF BIRDING HAS GROWN BEYOND our deepest expectations. This book represents the generous collaboration of many along the way; without their support, ideas, and commitment to birding, these pages could never have been assembled.

This project is the brainchild of Arthur Klebanoff, president of Scott Meredith Literary Agency and of the Roger Tory Peterson Institute, who first envisioned a beautifully appointed, comprehensive overview. The expertise and enthusiasm of our Rizzoli editor, Charles Miers, nurtured this book from the outset. His ideas and strong editorial hand are evident on every page. The preeminent American graphic designer Walter Bernard brought all of us together in the beginning, paving the way for such an auspicious combination of image, text, and design.

Robert Lewin, Laurie Simms, and Ellen Pedersen-Collard of Mill Pond Press deserve the deepest gratitude for their unflagging care in tending the artworks represented here. Mary Nygaard, their able assistant, rose to every conceivable occasion. Jane Kinne, Russ Kinne, and Nancy Carrizales of Comstock were critical in providing the finest examples of photography. Photographer Dennis Cowley reproduced the artwork with finesse. Linda Westervelt and Seymour Levin took the time to find additional images to enhance the book, images that would otherwise not have been seen. Architect Robert A. M. Stern gave us pictures of the Roger Tory Peterson Institute, which he so elegantly designed.

Many distinguished persons came forward to offer anecdotes and memories, to remind us of their perspective and passion for birds. In particular, Pamela Rasmussen of the Smithsonian Institution and Mary Ripley helped to encourage the foreword to fruition. Harry Foster, editor of the field guides at Houghton Mifflin, encouraged the project selflessly. Famed travelers Lars-Eric Lindblad and Sven-Olaf Lindblad gave generously of their time and energy. Paul Benke, executive director of the Roger Tory Peterson Institute, and his staff have been a continual source of support and knowledge.

The execution of such a complex project called upon the efforts of many, above and beyond any standard call of duty. At Rizzoli, the editorial and production contributions of Jen Bilik, Rose Scarpetis, and Elizabeth White moved the project through its many phases, and we thank Sandra Goroff-Mailly for her promotional insights. Jessica Simmons was a right hand to the design of the book; her organizational skills, design talent, and commitment are inestimably appreciated. Elaine Lillis and Jeannette Speirs gave tireless assistance, graciously addressing every need to bring this project to completion.

Finally, we thank our families for their loving support and patience. Our gratitude goes to Virginia Marie Peterson, whose contributions, expertise, and guidance were invaluable in giving form to this book. Jennifer Houser Hoglund displayed enormous understanding during the long absences and late nights entailed in completing this creation.

— Roger Tory Peterson and Rudy Hoglund

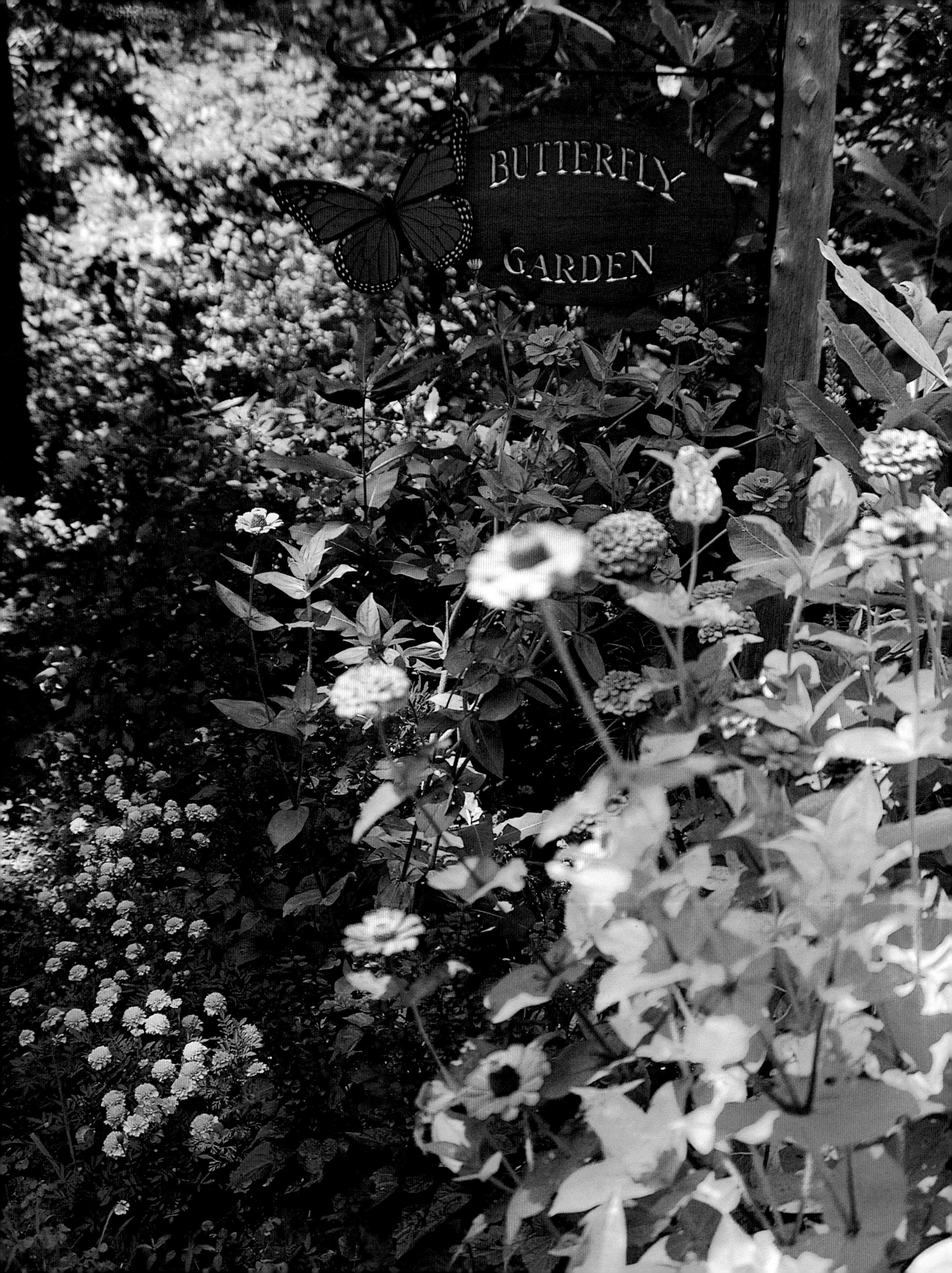
BUTTERFLY
GARDEN

CONTENTS

THE BUTTERFLY GARDEN

Opposite: Peterson has long been fascinated by butterflies, which he calls "flying flowers." His wife, Virginia Marie Peterson, created this butterfly garden in 1980. Planted so that it is visible from his studio window, the garden has attracted more than thirty species.

Five Harlequin Ducks fly low along 40-foot-high bluffs in Newfoundland. This pen-and-ink scratch-board drawing is the frontispiece for the 1955 book *Wild America,* an account by Peterson and British naturalist James Fisher about their 100-day, 30,000-mile trek through North America. The fantastically patterned Harlequins are known as "Lords and Ladies" to Newfoundlanders. In his guide to the birds of Eastern North America, Peterson tersely calls them "dark and bizarre."

FOREWORD

HAT IF THERE HAD BEEN NO ROGER TORY PETERSON? This question brings to mind imponderables such as whether we would all still be struggling to learn and identify birds using unwieldy tomes, or whether birds would have become the best-known animals in the world, as they now are. Peterson entered a world in which identification and study of birds was the exclusive realm of the specialist with a shotgun, and he transformed us into a world of watchers. The impact Peterson has had is incalculable; in providing the means for the popularization and refinement of bird-watching, he has immeasurably furthered bird study and the conservation movement worldwide. He enabled even the most untutored person to identify birds; he showcased the unparalleled beauty of birds in his painting and photography; and by getting millions of people interested he has helped to guarantee the survival of birds.

A man of many talents, but perhaps most celebrated for his instantly recognizable and attractive paintings, Roger Tory Peterson may have influenced more young bird artists and students than any other artist. Naturally, he set the standard in field guide illustration, having invented this art form! In fact, he is still at it, even as an octogenarian. His durability as a major figure in ornithology is unequalled; he has been contributing to this pursuit for over seventy years, and yet he has never failed to keep up with the times, undaunted by the new sophistication and competitiveness of birding and birders. Not only are birders indebted to Peterson, but many ornithologists owe their early interest in birds to Peterson. I remember well my first meeting with Roger in the Bird Division of the American Museum of Natural History, where he was diligently studying skins in the museum's collection for his bird guide; it was obvious at that time that this was no ordinary bird-watcher, but one could only guess at what was to come.

Peterson's modest little *A Field Guide to the Birds,* vintage 1934, is now an avidly sought collector's item; even so it still holds up to its intended purpose. Incredibly, this unassuming book was turned down by various publishers because of its untested format before Houghton Mifflin wisely took it on, a decision that has paid off to say the least. It has gone on to become a best seller, a status that has never diminished and has inspired a seemingly endless variety of other books in the Peterson series, now comprising more than sixty titles on many natural history subjects. Not only did he get the field guide idea off the ground, but Peterson was the first to demonstrate the real value of bird-song identification tapes, which are now considered essential to birding. We have Roger Tory Peterson to thank for making identification of all sorts of creatures possible, absorbing, even fun.

Roger, unlike so many others, inspires by example, not by preaching. He has traveled all the continents of the world in his quest, studying, painting, and filming birds everywhere he goes. Everything Peterson does becomes an event, and his doings are often imitated but not equaled: I remember an article celebrating his sighting of the Lesser Prairie Chicken, the final North American breeding species he needed for his life list of birds seen. He pioneered and popularized recreational birding and has headed teams of the finest birders (including the legendary Ted Parker) for record-breaking Big Days, the ultimate in competitive birding. Part of his energy is now channeled into the state-of-the-art, nonprofit Roger Tory Peterson Institute that he founded at his hometown in Jamestown, New York, and that has as its goal the nature education and motivation of children's mentors to ensure that the citizens of tomorrow are instilled with passion for and knowledge of nature. To this end, the institute sponsors nature workshops. awards, forums, publications, and exhibitions.

PETERSON'S ARTISTIC CONTRIBUTIONS, BESIDES ILLUMINATING THE pages of a number of field guides, grace the walls of ornithologists' and nature lovers' homes and offices around the country. They have been featured in many an exhibition, among them a celebration of the fiftieth anniversary of *A Field Guide to the Birds* held at the Smithsonian Institution in 1984, which attracted more than five million people. The Smithsonian exhibition was not limited to his paintings; excerpts from his writings and examples of his photography were also showcased in an effort to encompass the breadth of Peterson's talents and contributions. For these and so much more he has received a number of honors, degrees, and awards, including the Presidential Medal of Freedom, the highest award possible for an American civilian; he has also been nominated for a Nobel Peace Prize. I count it a high honor indeed to have had Roger Tory Peterson as associate and colleague for so long. It is fitting that we now celebrate his life's work to date; I won't say his career since I expect that Roger Tory Peterson still has more to contribute.

S. Dillon Ripley
Secretary Emeritus, Smithsonian Institution

A Keel-billed Toucan
from a pen-and-ink
drawing for *A Bird
Watcher's Anthology*,
Peterson's 1957
collection of writings
by prominent birders.
Some toucans have
bills that are longer
than their torsos.
The bills have teeth
toward the front
and are commonly
multicolored. The
Keel-billed, with five
colors on its bill, is
one of the world's
most radiant birds.

WATCHING THE
Birds

By WILLIAM ZINSSER

FOR MANY YEARS OUR FAMILY HAS HAD A SUMMER HOUSE ON THE SHORELINE OF southeastern Connecticut, overlooking a tidal marsh that has a generous allotment of egrets and herons and other wading birds. We also have a returning population of ospreys, which nest on the tall poles that people who live along the marsh have built to help them in their tenuous recovery from near disaster caused by DDT.

Among those native waders and divers, one day in the early 1960s, somebody spotted a flamingo, its gaudy pink plumage an affront to New England reticence, and we all hurried down to marvel at it and at whatever miscalculation had brought us a tropical bird that we didn't think got much farther north than Hialeah. Someone notified *The New York Times*, and the *Times* in turn called Roger Tory Peterson, who lives in nearby Old Lyme, and asked him to take a look. Peterson came over and certified our visitor, and the *Times* ran an article the next day, along with a picture of a flamingo. It wasn't our flamingo; it was a photograph from the files, but only another flamingo would have known the difference. In any case, there would be no doubting of the story itself—the *Times* had gone to the high priest.

Since that day I've often enjoyed knowing that we live in the same part of America as the man who made America a nation of birdwatchers. His *Field Guide to the Birds of North America* has been a best seller since 1934; for many families, looking something up in Peterson is as habitual as looking something

Opposite: The young Peterson, with field glasses, pad, and pencil, sketching at a summer camp in Maine. Peterson kept daily logs of his observations of birds from 1924 on. Above: A pen-and-ink drawing of a flock of Canada Geese from *A Field Guide to the Birds (Eastern North America)*.

"I have always been an artist and a naturalist, but that is true of most children to the age of twelve, when they give up those interests. From the age of twelve on I became serious. And since that age I have been accompanied by Roger Tory Peterson. My mother gave me a copy of his field guide for my birthday that year."

— **Robert Bateman**
Artist

up in Webster. My enjoyment took a new turn in 1992 when I watched a PBS documentary called "A Celebration of Birds," which summed up Peterson's life and work. It had so much beauty and accumulated wisdom that I wanted to know more about him—how he spends his days and what he thinks at the age of eighty-five. He agreed to a visit, and when we met I asked him if he remembered our flamingo. He said he did. How, I asked, did he think the stranger had gone so wrong?

"Birds have wings," he said, "and they use them."

PETERSON WAS METICULOUSLY PUTTING A FINAL DAB ON A bird painting when I arrived. He and his wife and collaborator, Virginia Marie Peterson, who prepares the detailed maps for his field guides, work in a spacious second-floor studio with huge windows that look over their wooded property, and while we talked he occasionally paused to notice a passing butterfly. "Roger gets bored if he can't see birds or butterflies," said Virginia Peterson, who solved the second half of that problem by planting a vivid "butterfly garden" outside her husband's studio. An extended family of six Wild Turkeys also dropped by the studio while I was there. They had become daily callers and consumers of the feed that Peterson sets out for them. "Two of the males are quite superior," he told me, pointing out some self-important behavior.

A tall man of Swedish immigrant stock, Peterson might be an elder in an Ingmar Bergman movie. The lock of white hair that used to fall over his forehead has receded—a loss he regrets. "It made me look like a hippie," he told

me with satisfaction; one theme that recurs in his recapitulation of his life is that he was always "sort of a rebel," taking the unmarked or unexpected path. The pale blue eyes that have served him so well are weaker, but his ear is still unusually good, though not good enough to hear a Cedar Waxwing. Hearing is central to the identification of birds, he believes. "When I used to walk through a rain forest with the late Ted Parker, who probably knew Latin American birds better than anyone, he looked at his feet and listened," he said.

At age eighty-five, Peterson puts in a working day that would tax a man of fifty. It runs to at least ten hours, starting with four hours of painting—labor so intensive that for relief he switches to writing or editing, or to his correspondence, or to photography. "My therapy, because it's not slavery, is photography," he told me. "I don't enjoy being out with birders today—they want to identify a bird and get on with it. I like to spend an hour with one bird. It may be a miserable little brown thing, but if it's cooperating I'll stay with it. I'll photograph any bird that will sit for me, even a house sparrow. How often do you see a good picture of a house sparrow?"

Opposite: Peterson, at age twelve or thirteen, with a butterfly net.
Above: Two American Wigeons on the wing, an oil on canvas done in Chautauqua County in western New York. This was Peterson's first oil painting. Despite some signs of tentativeness, it is a strong study.

Above: A mid-1920s watercolor vignette of a cat gazing up at a chickadee. This charming scene is conveyed with utmost directness and simplicity, hallmarks of the Peterson style in photography and writing as well as painting.
Opposite: An early 1920s brushed watercolor, pencil, and gouache drawing of a Common Snipe. Peterson had found the bird dead on a road near his home. Left unfinished by the teenaged Peterson, the drawing shows an almost oriental patterning. It has freshness and strength, but Peterson now calls it "much too fiddly and fine-tuned."

Peterson's first camera, acquired at the age of thirteen, was a Primo #9, which used glass plates and had bellows. He had taken a job delivering the morning paper in his hometown of Jamestown, New York, specifically to earn money to buy that camera to photograph birds. One result of getting up at four in the morning for his paper route was that he would fall asleep in school—an early component of his rebel image in matters of learning. (He also drew birds in the margins of his history book.) He has since worked with almost every kind of camera. "It's not that I copy my photographs when I paint," he explains, "but I do study them carefully."

Field trips to remote parts of the world are another release from painting. "Three months at the drawing board is all I can take," he said. "I try to go somewhere every three months and stay at least three weeks. I've been to Antarctica seventeen times. I love to visit Botswana—it's the most interesting country for wildlife in Africa. I want to go to the Arctic to look at polar bears. And to Elath, in Israel, for the hawk migration."

One pleasure of visiting new places is the chance to see new birds. Even after a lifetime of observing, Peterson has seen "scarcely more than 4,500" of the world's 9,000 species. Yet novelty isn't the main prize. "I'm impatient with birdwatchers who ask, 'Did you see any *good* birds today?' I like the idea of seeing any bird with a fresh eye. I may notice things I never noticed before. It could be something as simple as their reactions—how they react to me, or to each other. There's no such thing as a good bird or a bad bird. One of the rarest birds I could see is the Kagu, of New Caledonia, but at the other extreme I admire the House Sparrow, because it's a bird that manages to live on our terms, and we're the most difficult animal in the world."

The studio where we sat talking was a small outpost of the arts and sciences—easels, paints, paintbrushes, paintings, prints, maps, cameras, photographic equipment, tribal masks from many cultures, and shelves of reference books and journals—and it occurred to me that to think of Peterson as an ornithologist, as I always had, was to miss the point of a life that has been a mixture of many elements. Above all, I now realized, he is an artist. It is his painting that has made everything else work—has made his knowledge of birds accessible to millions and given him his authority as a writer, editor, photographer, educator, and conservationist, widely honored and consulted. He has become that enviable branch of American free enterprise, a personal industry, with its own building on his property, which serves as headquarters. I

17

wondered how such a lucky conjunction of interests—love of birds and love of painting—had been planted in that long-ago Jamestown, New York, boy.

"Very often a single bird will get a person started bird-watching," Peterson explained. "In my case it was a flicker that I saw when I was eleven, which I thought was dead—it was just a bundle of brown feathers. All of a sudden it exploded into life. That was the crucial moment of my life. I was overwhelmed by the contrast between something that was so vital and something I had taken for dead. Ever since that day I've felt that birds are the most vivid expression of life. Birds symbolize freedom, and I think that's why birdwatching is so important to so many people."

The person who got Peterson out and looking at birds was his seventh-grade teacher, Blanche Hornbeck. "We'll find out what they are," he recalled her saying. She thereby set him on a path so obsessive that, as he once wrote, "birds have been the focus of my existence; they have occupied my daily thoughts, filled my dreams, dominated my reading." Miss Hornbeck had organized a Junior Audubon Club, where children were given ten leaflets, each of which contained a description of a bird, a color plate of that bird, and an outline drawing to be colored in with crayons. The ten leaflets cost a dime.

"MISS HORNBECK SOON DECIDED THAT COLORING AN OUTLINED BIRD wasn't the way to learn how to draw," Peterson told me. "One day she brought in a portfolio of *The Birds of New York State,* by the great bird painter Louis Agassiz Fuertes. Each of us was given a small box of watercolors and a color plate from Fuertes's book to copy. I was given the blue jay, and that was my first bird painting. People often ask me what my favorite bird is, and I have to say it's the blue jay, though many people dislike its aggressive ways, and of course my other favorite is the flicker. Locally, here in Connecticut, my favorite is the osprey, and among sea birds it's the Wandering Albatross. My favorite bird family is the penguins. My Texas friends call me the King Penguin."

After high school Peterson temporarily put formal education behind him and got a job in Jamestown at the Union Furniture Company. The high school's other famous personage was Lucille Ball. "She was two years behind me, so I never dated her," Peterson said. "I was the school rebel and she was a school dropout who became Mrs. Middle America." At the furniture factory he decorated lacquered Chinese cabinets, and it was his unlikely good fortune

"Peterson's work taught me first to simplify. When I was a kid everything that had broad wings was called a chicken bird; but with the field guides, I could not only identify backyard birds at a distance, I was also inspired to go further into the woods."

— **Guy Coheleach**
Painter

that his first boss, a tyrannical Dutchman named Willem Dieperink von Langereis, was also his first artistic mentor. Von Langereis had been influenced by the decorative artist Aubrey Beardsley, who in turn had been influenced by Japanese woodcuts, and he instilled in his apprentice a Far Eastern sense of composition and design. Meanwhile, Peterson saved his money to go to New York City to attend his first meeting of the American Ornithologists Union, where one of his own paintings was on exhibit.

"It was a Kingbird," Peterson recalled, "and I had spent three weeks on it, painting every barbule of every feather, because I thought that was how Audubon painted. While I was at the meeting I was introduced to Fuertes. I was just seventeen, and he was the most influential of all American bird painters. Fuertes was the bridge to Audubon, because he brought life to the birds. He had studied architecture, and he thought like an architect—he knew how birds are put together. He knew that feathers follow form. Audubon's

Opposite: A mid-1920s charcoal sketch of a Cedar Waxwing.
Below: A wash and line drawing of a Common Yellowthroat feeding a nestling from the mid-1920s. In art, as in prose, Peterson makes clear the overwhelming psychic importance of birds in his life. He wrote in *Birds over America:* "Reluctant at first to accept the straitjacket of a world I did not comprehend, I finally, with the help of my hobby, made some sort of peace with society."

birds are relatively static because he wired his birds and stood them up to paint them. He also had a flamboyant personality. Audubon always expressed Audubon, whereas Fuertes always expressed the bird—the integrity of the species. Everyone was enamored of Fuertes's work. His field sketches were wonderful. He also handled transparent watercolor better than anybody else. That was his medium for years, until he met Allan Brooks, a Canadian, who told him that watercolors dry differently, and he was talked into gouache. He used gouache with great fidelity, and he was just moving toward Impressionism when I met him.

"Well, Fuertes looked at my Kingbird and he said, 'That's not quite the way to do it,' and he took me over to another painting, by the British artist Archibald Thorburn, to demonstrate a point about countershading. Then he reached into his pocket and took out a sable paintbrush. 'Take this brush,' he said. 'It's good for laying in background.' Fuertes also told me to send him my paintings. But I never did, because I wanted to wait until I was worthy of his time, and two years later he was killed in a car accident at a railroad crossing, at the age of fifty-three; his best Impressionist painting was still ahead of him. I also never used Fuertes's paintbrush. I had noticed that it had some flecks of

dried white paint on it, so I saved it as a memento; the master had used that brush. Then one day I lost it—it fell between some boards in the floor. Later I took up the boards to look for the brush and I found that a mouse had chewed off the bristles to make a nest. It taught me very early that everything in nature is related."

A T AGE EIGHTEEN, PETERSON MOVED TO NEW YORK, AT THE URGING of Von Langereis, to study art, first at the Art Students League and then at the National Academy of Design. That was the moment when he consciously chose art; the alternative had been to go to Cornell University to study biology. In New York he met nine high school boys from the Bronx who were avid birders and called themselves the Bronx County Bird Club. Their guru was Ludlow Griscom, a curator at the American Museum of Natural History, who was then pioneering the field technique of identifying birds through binoculars; almost everyone else still used a shotgun. "The club had two rules: You had to be good and you had to be from the Bronx," Peterson told me. "I was good, but I wasn't from the Bronx. But they finally had to take me in." He remembers those weekend walks under Griscom's strict mentorship as a pivotal chapter in his life: "We learned all about field marks from Griscom. He set the new standards. He represented the new ornithology."

At the same time, Peterson was intensively studying art. "One of my great teachers at the Art Students League," he said, "was Kimon Nikolaides, who taught drawing from models and whose book *The Natural Way to Draw* is a classic to this day. My approach to field sketching came from him; I've still got a lot of Nikolaides in me. At that time I was interested in the Impressionists' quick fall of light—the idea of form as created by light." Another of his teachers at the League was John Sloan, a star of the Ashcan School of painting and a master of social realism. "Sloan was then in his crosshatch period, and he said, 'There's no such thing as a cast shadow'—which I couldn't agree with. But I did get color relationships from him: the principle that cool colors recede and warm colors move toward you."

Sloan and his fellow voyagers in the onrushing movements of modern art despised academic painting and told Peterson that to enroll at the National Academy would be "eternal damnation." Risking hellfire, he signed up anyway and stayed three years, discovering that his studies with such academic masters as Edmund Dickinson and Raymond Neilson were perfect training for a young man who aspired to paint the natural world. Although realism was the main goal for a naturalist, it could be achieved, Peterson learned, not only by detail but also by the methods of Impressionism—the manipulation of light.

Meanwhile he took all of New York City as his textbook. "It was an astonishingly rich habitat for him," Joseph Kastner writes in *World of Watchers,* his enjoyable history of the American passion for birds, "and over the years Peterson birded it devotedly, finding Bonaparte's Gulls at the 92nd Street sewer outlet in Brooklyn, watching chickadees migrating down Seventh Avenue, counting curlews flying over Greenwich Village, spotting a woodcock on the ledge of the old General Motors Building and a Peregrine Falcon from a window in the Time-Life Building. On a very foggy morning, with Central Park full of confused fall migrants, he saw half a dozen Scarlet Tanagers in one tree and four Rose-breasted Grosbeaks in another, five species of thrushes, a Florida Gallinule (Common Moorhen), and an Audubon's 'Bimaculated' Duck. He listened to migrant warblers at night from the top of the RCA Building and tracked down a Hermit Thrush that had migrated into a florist shop at 63rd Street and Madison Avenue." He also made weekly trips to the Bronx Zoo to draw its birds. "There were two that I constantly drew," he told me. "They were the Shoebilled Stork and the Eagle Owl, which is like our Great Horned Owl. I drew them because they never moved a muscle. They would sit for ten minutes at a time."

Thus Peterson was poised to become a "painterly" artist of birds, a follower of Audubon and Fuertes, when, in 1934, after several years of teaching art and natural history at the Rivers School near Boston, he hit upon the formula that would change his life and severely constrain his painting style. Attempting to prepare a field guide of his own, he was annoyingly reminded of one he had grown up using: Frank Chapman's *Birds of Eastern North America,* which was published in 1895 and had been a bible of birdwatchers ever since.

"Chapman would describe a bird from its beak to its tail," Peterson told me, "but wouldn't give you the one clue you needed to identify it quickly. If the bird was a robin, he'd start by telling you about the white spot above and below the eye, and about the white throat streaked with black, and halfway through his account you'd learn that the bird has a red breast. I thought that was a confusing system for the average birder, and I wanted to develop a better one. I'm basically a person who likes to simplify and not amplify.

"I remembered that when I was a boy I enjoyed a novel called *Two Little Savages,* by Ernest Thompson Seton, in which there's a young man named Yan who can't identify ducks he sees flying overhead. One day he finds himself looking at some ducks in a showcase. The ducks are all in their uniforms, easy to identify, and Yan thinks, 'If I can identify them in this showcase I ought to be able to identify them in the field.' I realized that that had been my first

glimpse of the idea I was groping for in my field guide, and that's how I went ahead and did it. I grouped birds that look alike and therefore might be mistaken for each other, instead of grouping them by species, and I painted them in similar positions so that they could be compared. I made my paintings schematic and two-dimensional, and I drew little arrows to point out the 'field marks' that are the main information you need to identify a bird. Those arrows were my invention."

The result was an innovative book submitted by an unknown artist in a Depression year, and it was rejected by four publishers before Houghton Mifflin took a chance on a printing of 2,000, stipulating, as a financial hedge, that Peterson would receive no royalties on the first 1,000 copies. That was the last time Peterson was considered a gamble. The first printing sold out in a week, propelled by a review in *The New York Herald Tribune*, which, weighing the bird guide against the current run of novels, said it was the book most likely to be remembered in ten years. "That surprised me," Peterson recalls, "because I thought it was relatively crude, compared with what it later became." In any case, the six decades since 1934 have caused nothing but gratitude at bookstores that sell the *Field Guide* and its almost fifty companion volumes, which operate on the same principle, identifying such natural forms as butterflies, moths, beetles, wildflowers, shells, and rocks and minerals. Peterson is the series editor.

"For years his *Field Guide* stood alone, the one guide everyone used, the unchallenged best seller," Joseph Kastner writes. "In the prosperity that came after the war, bird watchers multiplied . . . and other guides were published, all adopting the Petersonian philosophy of emphasizing recognizable field marks, though not copying his technique." Today close to a million general bird guides are sold every year in the United States, plus innumerable local, regional, and state guides, how-to books on bird photography, and manuals on birding techniques and field equipment.

But Peterson's was the guide that launched the new era. In the year of its birth, 1934, there were probably 400,000 birdwatchers in the world; today there are 40 million. "More than any single man," Kastner observed, "Peterson pushed birds into the American consciousness." To Paul Ehrlich and David Dobkin, authors of *The Birder's Handbook*, Peterson's guide is "a monument to his ability to paint the very essence of a bird. [But] his greatest contribution to the preservation of biological diversity has been in getting tens of millions of people outdoors with decent field guides in their pockets."

"In his nostalgic moments Roger tells me that the stories we worked on together at LIFE more than half a century ago were a crucial turning point in his career. The editor had remarked that bird watching was becoming popular—what could we do about it? I said I had a friend who could become the most important bird artist since Audubon."

— Joseph Kastner
Editor

Peterson himself sees his guide as the bridge between the "shotgun school" of ornithology that prevailed well into this century, when a naturalist who wanted to identify a bird would simply shoot it down, and modern birding, with its respect for nature and its use of sophisticated binoculars, cameras, and optical equipment. Still, fame can be capricious. "One problem with being a teacher is that you never know whether anything has rubbed off," he said when I remarked on the prodigious success of his book. It turned out that Blanche Hornbeck, his seventh-grade teacher, took a summer course in ornithology at Cornell a few years before she retired, and for its text the class was given Roger Tory Peterson's *Field Guide to the Birds.* "That was the first time she knew that her freckle-faced kid had written it."

Today Peterson is still stretching his wings—every barbule of every feather—doing spacious bird paintings of the kind that might have put his

Indian
Adjutant

Early pencil studies of waterfowl sketched on the lake at the Bronx Zoo (opposite) and a Marabou Stork with Boat-billed Herons (left) also done at the zoo. The artist's modus operandi of arraying repeated smaller figures on a sketchpad seems to prefigure the famous layouts of the bird guides.

28

work in art galleries long ago if he hadn't turned pedagogical. "You get known for a certain thing because you do it well," he told me, "but I'd like to prove to myself that I can do paintings that have an Audubonesque quality. And I'm still after that Impressionist fall of light; I can't say I've got it right yet. There's a difference between illustration, which is a teaching device, as in my field guides, and painting that's evocative of your emotions. I'm envious of certain painters who have achieved that."

He took down a book of Audubon's painting and a book of Fuertes's paintings and showed me aspects of both men's work that he would like to incorporate into his own paintings. He spoke approvingly of Edward Lear, whose great bird paintings have been usurped in fame by his great nonsense poems, and of various modern painters whose work he admires: Robert Bateman, Keith Shackleton, Guy Coheleach, Don Eckelberry, Lars Jonsson, and Peter Scott.

"*I* CALL MY WORK 'MIXED-MEDIA,'" PETERSON SAID, "BECAUSE MY MAIN purpose is to instruct, and I'm always thinking in terms of reproduction. I seldom paint in just one medium. I may start with transparent watercolors, then I go to gouache, then I give it a protective coat of acrylic, then I go over that with acrylics or a touch of pastel, or colored pencil, or pencil or ink—anything that will do what I want. I seldom do a straight watercolor; I can't handle it accurately. Right now I'm straddling—trying to add a bit more detail without losing the simplified effect. Over the years so many people have become familiar with the straight profile of my birds that they've begun to want something more: the look of feathers, or a more three-dimensional feeling. So I'm moving from simplification to amplification in cases where I think it will help."

To master one art of such complexity would seem to be achievement enough for one lifetime. But Peterson is also a master of two other arts: photography and writing. Along with painting, they have doubled and tripled his influence.

"I've always enjoyed photography because there's an immediacy to it," he says. "It's like hunting, but you're not taking life; you're recording life. Bird photography isn't just point-and-shoot. You have to 'see' a picture and compose it. It also has an ethical component, because you're intruding on an animal. A good nature photographer practically lives with the animal until the animal accepts him.

"One way of not intruding is to use a lens long enough so that the animal isn't panicked. I mainly use 600-millimeter lenses, or, in the case of flying

When Peterson was a young art student in New York City, admission to the Bronx Zoo was free six days a week, 25 cents on Thursdays. To paint in peace, without kibbitzers over his shoulder, Peterson usually went on Thursdays. And he usually painted the Great Horned Owl (opposite, in watercolor and gouache), the Eagle Owl, or the Shoebilled Stork. They were fascinating and ideal models for painters: they rarely moved at all.

This page: Dutchman's Breeches and Pitcher Plant. Opposite page: Hepatica and Jack-in-the-Pulpit. These india ink drawings for the book *Wild America* are strikingly bold and dark. Though some see echoes of Francis Lee Jaques here,

Peterson points to the influence of Aubrey Beardsley, a favorite of his first boss, Von Langereis, who taught him to paint designs on lacquered cabinets when Peterson was a teenager in Jamestown, New York.

birds, a 300-millimeter lens. I like to photograph birds from a car; I rest my camera on the window for support. To a bird, the car is just a big animal with round legs. But if you step out of it they won't accept you; people are a menace. I also like to go into the field and sit on a stool and cloak myself in a portable blind called Leafoflage, which I can set up very quickly—in about two minutes. It's cut in patterns that look like moving leaves and it has a lot of holes. I do my observing and shoot my pictures through the holes."

In his seventy years behind a camera Peterson graduated from his boyhood Primo to the bulky Auto-Graflex, progressed to the more compact Speed-Graphic, to the still smaller Swedish Hasselblad and Japanese Bronica, then to the Leica, the Pentax, and the Olympus, and finally settled on the automatic Canons and Nikons that are his favorites today. Of all the technical improvements in that long lineage he considers auto-focus the biggest blessing, not only because his eyes are poorer and his reflexes slower but because birds are seldom at rest.

"If you can get the bird in your viewfinder, the camera will do the rest," he explained. He is also fond of the fill-in flash, because "film never sees as much as you see. The human eye sees detail in the shadows. But the fill-in flash enables the camera to pick up that detail. You just can't do good bird photography without good equipment." Equipment, however, is only technology. "Many people think good equipment makes it easy—they're deceived into thinking the camera does it all," Peterson said. "But as a photographer you bring your eye and a sense of composition to the process, and also warmth; you don't shoot pictures at high noon, for instance, or at the beginning or the end of the day. You're also mindful of the quality of light—a thin overcast can do nice things. Knowledge of the animal is also a tremendous help: anticipating what a bird will do. You can anticipate such activities as a feeding frenzy, when birds feed on fish traveling in small groups. Feeding frenzies are important to a photographer because one of the basic things birds do is eat, and they'll put up with you a lot longer if they're eating. In fact, they'll often ignore you."

All these gains in judgment and technology converged for Peterson in 1994, when he made a two-week field trip to Venezuela and shot 120 rolls of film, visiting two huge tracts that have been set aside as biological reserves for birdwatchers and other nature-oriented people. "I took along a new Canon 600-millimeter long lens," he said, "which has a doubler that gets 1200. No bird can possibly escape me now. At one site, the Llanos, a plain that covers thousands of square miles, I photographed the hoatzin, a very strange bird that always manages to keep a few branches between itself and you; I had never

From *Wild America*, a pen-and-ink scratchboard sketch of gloomy Fort Jefferson in the Dry Tortugas, seventy miles off Key West. One of the most bird-rich sites in North America, this coral atoll is home to 100,000 or more Sooty Terns. It is also the final resting place for thousands of exhausted migrants, which land there to rest—but eventually starve. The atoll has no water or food source, except fish and other birds.

been able to get a picture of it before. At El Cedral I saw hundreds of thousands of Whistling Ducks and some Scarlet Ibis, which is the one I wanted most. This trip brings my bird photography up to date. It's my best work so far. My really best work is still to come."

Writing is the third of Peterson's important skills. He writes very well. How he put that skill to use in preparing the *Field Guide* was deftly analyzed by Joseph Kastner:

> His mental discipline enabled him to ignore unneeded detail . . . and to eliminate what other guides had always put in. He was not concerned with being complete, just comprehensible, and he had developed, with no tutoring, a laconic writing style that matched his spare drawings. There was little room for discussion in his *Guide,* which allowed only a few lines of text for each bird, rarely more than 20 in which to give the bird's popular and scientific names, the field marks of male and female, tick off similar species and how they differed, give the calls and songs, the habitat and range. Peterson raised the use of the word "only" to high art—few prose writers have gotten so much mileage out of it—so that the bird watcher could dismiss all irrelevant differences from his mind. For example, the oldsquaw is the "only sea duck combining much white on the body and unpatterned dark wings." The common screech owl is "our only small eastern owl with ear tufts." The barn swallow is the "only native swallow that is truly 'swallow-tailed.'" His classic description was that of the male goldfinch: "The only small yellow bird with black wings."

IN A LEISURELY FORMAT PETERSON'S STYLE IS NO LESS WINNING. A PLEASANT example is *Wild Islands,* one of four books he is now writing in his spare moments. ("I'm trying for a hundred and fourteen," he told me. "That's how many years it will take me to finish all the books and painting and photography I want to do.") The book describes certain islands he has visited that attract ornithologists, such as the Falklands, the Galápagos, and South Georgia. "Islands concentrate birds," Peterson said, adding that not all islands are necessarily in the sea. "They can also be in the desert; the Okavango delta in Botswana's Kalahari desert has hundreds of little islands where birds congregate."

Typical of the narrative vigor in *Wild Islands* is an account of a trip to the Dry Tortugas many years ago to visit the largest colony of terns in the United States. Part historian, part scientist, part tour guide, Peterson is the very model of a travel writer:

> On the 10th of May we docked at Fort Jefferson, the slave-built fortress that dominates the Tortugas, the sandy atoll 70 miles off Key West in the Gulf of

Mexico. The hexagonal fortress with its endless wall 50 feet high and eight feet thick was said to have cost a dollar for every one of its 42 million bricks, and that was when a dollar was worth many times what it is today. The purpose of the fort was to guard the sea approaches to the Gulf from the threat of British expansion. But the British never came except as tourists.

When James Fisher and I rowed the dinghy across the channel to Bush Key, a dark, noisy cloud of sooty terns boiled up and protested deafeningly, but soon they settled. They were very tame. For hours we sat on the beach watching the birds squabbling over the tiny territories around the scrapes that held their single eggs. Bodies flexed, wings held out and slightly opened, necks arched, they bowed like bookends opposing each other, touched bills, flared up in emotion, suddenly to break off and preen; they fiddled with their egg, billing it into a more comfortable position against the incubation patch.

John James Audubon saw these tropical seabirds in 1832. He stayed in Key West all summer, painting portraits for his *Birds of America,* and while

there he visited the Tortugas on the revenue cutter *Marion*. The first lieutenant told Audubon that the sooties and noddies were "on their respective breeding grounds by the millions." Indeed, these two species are the most populous terns of the tropical seas; on some islands in the Indian Ocean there are sooty colonies of over a million nests. But it is difficult to guess, from Audubon's account, just what numbers he found. Bird Key, where Audubon saw the biggest colony, no longer exists. It started to erode in 1928 and disappeared entirely 10 years later, during the hurricane of 1938. Since then the birds have used Bush Key, closer to the fort.

"At Bird Key," Audubon wrote, "we found a party of Spanish eggers from Havana. They had already laid in a cargo of about eight tons of the eggs of this [sooty] tern and the noddy. On asking them how many they supposed they had, they answered that they never counted them, even when selling them, but disposed of them at 75 cents a gallon, and that one turn to market sometimes produced upwards of $200, while it took only a week to sail backwards and forwards to collect their cargo."

A splendid array of tropical birds from New Guinea, South America, Cuba, Australia, South Asia, and Africa adorn this oil on board painting for Peterson's book *The World of Birds*.

It is mainly through his writing that Peterson has been an advocate for conservation. "I'm not an activist in the sense of bothering my Congressman," he told me. "I'm an opinion-maker in my writing and my painting. I'm a publicizer. I like to give people information, and over the years I've written a great many articles for magazines. Activists sometimes work on information that's not valid."

Typical of Peterson's publicizing efforts are his seventeen trips to Antarctica, starting in 1957, when Lars-Eric Lindblad initiated tours to that continent, and he has been going back on Lindblad ships ever since, most recently in 1993, to photograph penguins and other birds. "But I was also watching such things as pollution," he says, "and over the years we've made them clean up the bases by calling attention to how the environment was being damaged and how much wildlife depends on it. Eight nations keep bases there. I used to talk about that and show my films of Antarctica on Audubon Lecture Tours, which were booked into two hundred cities, or I'd lend my slides to other Audubon lecturers. One result is that today when tourists go to the Antarctic and see something that's out of kilter they make a fuss about it."

The National Audubon Society is only one of many preservation groups that Peterson has been associated with, as an officer or a board member or a consultant. Others include the Sierra Club, the World Wildlife Fund, and the National Wildlife Federation, whose annual series of "wildlife stamps," born in 1937 during the presidency of the stamp collector Franklin D. Roosevelt, has involved Peterson for more than 50 years as an artist, designer, and editor. "Every year in my studio," he once explained, "we lay out all the new stamps that have been submitted and arrange them selectively, keeping in mind color balance, subject matter, and regional representation. We try to have something for every wildlife-oriented person: the birdwatcher, the angler, the sportsman, the gardener, etc. Making it jell is like working out a jigsaw puzzle or playing a

A Wild Turkey going to roost in a pine, in a pen-and-ink sketch from Peterson's book *The Bird-Watcher's Anthology*. Peterson and Herbert Bradt, a professional turkey raiser, camped out under camouflage in Arizona's Chiricahua Mountains to observe how Wild Turkeys behave at nightfall.

had been fashionable to look down as important as the literate writers world. Can anyone remember Turkey?"

— **Roger Tory Peterson**

game of chess. The program has been enormously successful, raising millions of dollars and making the National Wildlife Federation the largest and most influential organization concerned with the conservation of wildlife in this country. The stamps made it happen."

But the organization that now engages his thoughts and emotions is a newcomer: the Roger Tory Peterson Institute of Natural History, founded in 1984 in his boyhood town of Jamestown, New York, where he saw the flicker that started it all. Inspired by Peterson's life's work, the institute takes as its mission "to inform society about the natural world through the study and teaching of natural history." In its handsome new building, designed by the architect Robert A. M. Stern, it conducts a busy program of teacher workshops, scholarships, annual national forums on issues of concern to nature educators, publications for teachers and parents, and awards for teaching excellence. In the past two years 1,500 elementary and middle-school teachers have participated in its workshops.

"EXCEPT IN THE CASE OF JOHN JAMES AUDUBON IT had been fashionable to look down on nature painters," Peterson said. "They weren't taken seriously unless they put people or animals in their paintings, and the animal had to be related to humans in some way: a stag rising in position to be shot, or a pheasant rising in front of a hunter's dogs. But painters are as important as the literate writers in presenting the grandeur of the natural world. Can anyone remember what Audubon *wrote* about the Wild Turkey?"

"Peterson is to the world of birding in the twentieth century what Stanislavsky was to those of us in theater. When I first became interested in birds, it was to Peterson's guides that I turned . . . and Roger Tory Peterson made a credible birder out of this actor."

— Jane Alexander
Actress and Chairman of The National Endowment for the Arts

Otus Petersoni (the Cinnamon Screech-Owl) was identified in the eastern Andes and described by two American ornithologists in the 1970s. They named the bird in honor of Peterson. This made the bird an unusually satisfying subject for the painter. He is pleased too that an owl bears his name. "I've always had an affinity for owls," he said on hearing of the naming.

Today the validity of nature painting is being recognized by some art critics, Peterson said. He credits this to the environmental movement and to the new awareness of the sanctity and fragility of nature. "I go halfway back to Audubon," he said, "so I have a feeling for the changes that have taken place." In his boyhood, he reminded me, every kid with a slingshot would shoot birds, and many species had been killed off or brought close to extermination by hunters who slaughtered them for their plumes, or to sell to restaurants, or for sport. The good news, which he has lived long enough to see, is that a number of species have made a comeback from their narrow escape, helped by a citizenry that now takes an active role in protecting birds and their threatened habitats.

"This is a time of enormous change in people's thinking," Peterson said. "The attitude of people towards birds has changed the attitude of birds towards people. Even crows are becoming tamer. Gulls have increased—they're the cleanup crew at garbage dumps. People have begun to see that life itself is important—not just ourselves, but all life. The older I get, the more I feel the interconnectedness of things all over the world."

His own conversation had been just such a web of connecting threads. When he talked about birds he often ended up talking about butterflies and insects, worrying about how recent shifts in the weather would affect their ancient cycles of dependency and migration, or how such human intrusions as pesticides and the destruction of forests and beaches would alter an equilibrium that is already delicate enough. "The spray that kills the gypsy moth also kills a hundred other things that you never hear about," he said. "Birds are a litmus of the environment. If something is out of balance they reflect it very quickly, so we should keep watch and take action to correct what has gone wrong."

As both a watcher and a watchman of birds, I realized, Peterson the man would never get out from under Peterson the book. He was still its pris-

R. T. Peterson—

oner. "My guide to the birds of Eastern North America is fourteen years old in its present edition," he said, "and I'm now revising it for a fifth edition. There's a lot that needs to be done. Many of my renditions could be improved. My wife Ginny and I have also got to recheck the range of all species. Many birds are extending their range, so there are new species I ought to add, like the Shiny Cowbird, which has come into Florida from Cuba and the West Indies, and the Mexican Crow, which has turned up at the Brownsville dump. You'll find pelicans much farther north now. The Jackdaw has been appearing in the Maritime Provinces.

"Some birds have also changed their nesting habits in adaptation to man's encroachments. The Common Tern used to be a beach nester; now more and more are beginning to nest off the beach, so that's where birdwatchers should look for them. The Least Tern has taken to nesting on top of shopping malls—a few years ago there were a thousand pair on the roof of the Singing River Mall in Gautier, Mississippi. Mockingbirds are particularly fond of malls—they like the planting, especially the multiflora rose; its tiny hips are small enough for them to swallow. Mockingbirds also enjoy the bustle of shopping malls. They sit there and direct the traffic."

FOR THE NEW EDITION THE PETERSONS ARE ALSO TAKING A FRESH look at every state. "Birds don't observe state lines," he said, and state lines in turn often don't observe what lies within their borders. "Texas should really be five states. The only true part of Texas is the Edwards Plateau, around Austin; it has birds specific to that region. The area around Beaumont is more like Louisiana. Around Amarillo it's more like the Plains. West of the Pecos it's mountains—true West—and Brownsville is rather like Mexico." Peterson is also adding birds to the guide that are found in the Rio Grande delta, a region not included in the previous eastern edition.

The talk turned to editors' demands and printers' deadlines and publishers' schedules, and I asked Peterson why he couldn't just put all that behind him now and retire to what he really wants to do: painting and photography.

"It's a responsibility that I hate to avoid," he replied. "A lot of people are dependent on me."

He got up to check on his Wild Turkeys, watching them through a crack in a curtain. "I don't want to open that curtain," he said, "because it was closed when they first came here, and if I changed anything it would upset them."

I asked Peterson if he had shown me everything. "Would you like to see my collection of birds?" he asked. I said I certainly would. He led me down an outside staircase to a cellar door, which he unlocked, ushering me into a basement full of cabinets and drawers—the familiar furniture of scientific storage, reminiscent of every small college museum that never got modernized. Darwin might have used such drawers.

"I've got 2,000 specimens down here that I use for research," Peterson said. "Most of them are around 100 years old, and they're still useful." He pulled open a drawer and took out a bird and showed me its tag: ACORN WOODPECKER, APRIL 10, 1882. "Think of it: this bird is 112 years old," he said. He opened some other drawers and gently held several other late Victorians for me to ponder—a link to the presidency of Grover Cleveland.

In another part of the basement Peterson showed me further marvels of storage and classification: files containing more than 100,000 photographic slides. Cans of old movie film, which he once used to illustrate his lectures, sat on nearby shelves. "At least 10,000 of my slides are of Ring-bill Gulls," he said. "I've continued to photograph them over the years for purposes of comparison of film and equipment, because they always come back here to the mouth of the Connecticut River. They patronize a restaurant in Old Saybrook called the Dock 'n' Dine."

Leaving Peterson to his Wild Turkeys and his butterfly garden, I asked him: "What do you know at eighty-five that you didn't know when you were seventy?"

"What I've come to know," he said, "is how much I don't know."

"About painting?" I asked.

"No," he said. "About birds."

Roger Tory Peterson in 1993, with a Scrub Jay and a copy of his 1990 Eastern field guide in hand.

"KING PENGUIN" AND OTHER STORIES

I REMEMBER BIRDING WITH ROGER TORY PETERSON—OR THE "KING PENGUIN," to refer to him by his bird name—on a small plot of land called High Island, which is on the Texas coast down the line from Galveston. It is a remarkable place to look for birds in the spring migratory season, especially warblers, because in effect High Island is a large hummock rising out of the marshlands— the first point of land the birds see as they complete their exhausting flight across the Gulf of Mexico. They plump down in the welcome groves of oak and hackberry. Years ago it was possible to sight as many as twenty-five different warblers during an afternoon's walk through the small sanctuary. Alas, with the destruction of breeding habitats, especially the rain forests, the number of different species declines every year. Still it is a popular place for birders; each tree has two or three birders staring up, sometimes many more if a rare species has been spotted up in the branches.

On this particular day the word got around that King Penguin was in the sanctuary. Someone recognized him. Instantly he became the center of attention. I don't believe that the arrival in the treetops of such a rare sighting as, say, a Cape May Warbler, would have unfocused their attention. Some of the more forward members of a women's birding club came up and introduced themselves, eyes shining. He signed a few copies of their bird guides. Others, more contained, stayed their distance, looking at him over bushes or from around the side of a tree, some peering at him through their binoculars. That was the sight I would remember—the glint of binoculars, ten yards away, so close that surely only a part of Peterson's face, the side of his nose, his eyebrows, the pale blue eyes themselves, would have filled the viewer's field of vision. Whatever, it was a sight they would obviously treasure. It was also a measure of Peterson's influence and fame that he could create such a commotion in that small wooded glen.

— **George Plimpton**
Author

I ONCE BIRDED WITH PETERSON IN THE GALÁPAGOS. ROGER WAS WEARING A Panama to shield his head from the blazing sun. A Darwin Finch chose to land on the hat and, as Roger and I chatted, the bird turned its head from me to him and back to me like a spectator at a tennis match. What a time not to have a camera—a Darwin Finch perched atop Roger Tory Peterson and occasionally bending over the hat's rim and peering at him upside down.

— Roger Caras
Author

HOW MUCH WILL THIS NEW PETERSON FIELD GUIDE COST?" ASKED JUDGE ROBERT Walcott, president of the Massachusetts Audubon Society at a dinner party in 1934. "$2.50," I replied. "Paul," he said firmly, looking at me with judicial authority over his half-moon glasses, "the Reed guides cost only 50 cents." I subsided. A year later, when I was again at the Walcott's, the judge immediately inquired, "Have you heard about that wonderful new Peterson field guide? Every ornithologist has one in his pocket." "Yes," I replied. I had heard of it.

Birders at Cape May, New Jersey, one of North America's premier points for watching birds.

— Paul Brooks
First editor of the Peterson field guides

"Roger Tory Peterson has furthered the study, appreciation, and protection of birds the world over. And he has done more. He has impassioned thousands of Americans, and has awakened in millions across this land a fondness for nature's other two-legged creatures."

— **Jimmy Carter**
39th President of the United States

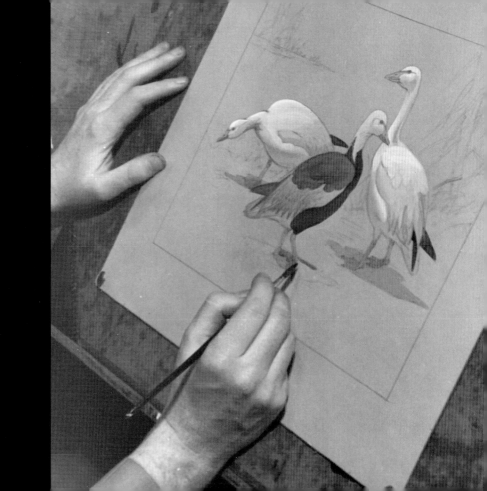

THE PAINTINGS

TWO GREAT BIRD PAINTERS HELPED SHAPE PETERSON'S ART: JOHN JAMES Audubon, who forever changed the nation's perceptions of bird life, and Louis Agassiz Fuertes, the master bird painter of the day when Peterson was growing up.

Audubon's influence is harder to trace. The mature Peterson painted life-sized birds against a background of a specific flower or tree, just as Audubon did. But Peterson's "Audubonesque" paintings seem elegant and genteel when compared with the writhing, romantic, highly dramatic action that Audubon poured into many of his watercolors. Peterson could produce drama, as he did in his painting of a hummingbird about to devour a moth (page 72). But this has been rare. Though he favored sensuous painting, Peterson has almost always avoided "Audubonesque" action.

Peterson has always been careful to make respectful comments about Audubon's pioneering work, but he has left no doubt that his stronger respect and allegiance are to Fuertes. He once wrote: "Those who really know birds insist there is more latent life in a Fuertes bird, composed and at rest, than in an Audubon bird wildly animated."

So Peterson has worked to bring out the essence of birds as Fuertes did, sometimes in close-up bird portraits, sometimes in Fuertes-like paintings of birds active in their environment. Occasionally, these works seem influenced by the brilliant dioramas at the Museum of Natural History in New York (see Peterson's Golden Eagle; opposite). And once, at least, the environment in a Peterson painting has seemed to dominate its birds—the Whooping Cranes (opposite)—but in general he has tended to avoid painting birds as merely part of a broad natural scene. He says of the Whooping Cranes painting, "The more complex you make a painting, the more likely that the work loses force."

As a painter of birds, Peterson is a superb craftsman with only one overriding problem: the enormous labor of the field guides has pulled him away from "painterly" art. The work of creating and revising the guide artwork has trapped him, Peterson says, and "led many people to think that the decoy-like drawings were my basic style."

Crested Caracara, by John James Audubon. Watercolor, pastel, and graphite on paper. 1831.

Eastern Phoebe, by Louis Agassiz Fuertes. Watercolor. Undated.

Adult Golden Eagle, with Immature in Flight, from studies done in Wyoming. 1976.

This 1959 oil painting of Whooping Cranes, a species almost extinct at the time, was commissioned by the National Audubon Society as a gift for its retiring president, John Baker. It is a rare Peterson work in which nature itself, and not birds, seems to dominate the canvas. The birds are shown on their remote and almost impenetrable breeding grounds in the Northwest Territories.

"*In my mind's eye I can see Roger as a perennial Norseman, striding along cliff edges or on rocky promontories washed by pounding surf, white hair tossing in the wind, binoculars clutched at the ready, he represents an undying enthusiasm for all the works of nature.*"

— S. Dillon Ripley
Secretary Emeritus, Smithsonian Institution

Atlantic Puffins on the Maine Coast. Mixed media. 1979.

Brown Pelicans. Watercolor, gouache, and acrylics. 1990.

"Birds don't reciprocate your interest. . . . They can certainly live without me, but I don't think I could live without birds."

— **Roger Tory Peterson**

Florida Scrub Jays. Watercolor and gouache. 1958.

American Kestrels. Mixed media. 1958.   *Peregrine Falcons. Mixed media. c. 1960.*

"We are too close to ourselves, much of the time, to see our proper relation to the natural world, on which we depend for survival. Watching birds and other animals seems to clarify my perspective."

— **Roger Tory Peterson**

White Gyrfalcons, Greenland. Mixed media. 1979.

Snowy Owls. Transparent watercolor and gouache. 1976.

Roadrunners with Prickly Pear Cacti (from a study done in Tucson, Arizona). Mixed media. 1976.

Barn Owls with English Ivy (from studies done in the Bronx). Mixed media. 1975.

Male and Female Northern Cardinals with Multiflora Rose. Mixed media. 1973.

"*Birds are far more than cardinals and orioles to brighten the garden. They are indicators of the environment—a sort of ecological litmus.*"

— **Roger Tory Peterson**

© Roger Tory Peterson '73

> *"The Blue Jay is a favorite; it was the first bird I drew. When I was eleven I copied a colorplate by Fuertes."*

— **Roger Tory Peterson**

Barn Swallows with Phragmites.
Watercolor and gouache. 1973.

Blue Jays with Autumn Oak Leaves.
Mixed media. 1976.

63

American Robin with Dogwood. Mixed media. 1978.

"To want to protect wildlife and the habitats that support it, people first have to know what they are protecting. Beginning with birds and later expanding to everything from trees to tadpoles, Roger Tory Peterson has made natural history accessible."

— Robert McCracken Peck
The Academy of Natural Sciences of Philadelphia

Wood Thrush with Violets. Mixed media. 1973. Following pages: Ring-necked Pheasants with Black-eyed Susans. Watercolor, gouache, and acrylics. 1978. 65

© Roger Tory Peterson '77

© Roger Tory Peterson-'78

Rose-breasted Grosbeaks. Mixed media. 1978.

Northern Mockingbird Doing a Wing Display. Mixed media. 1978.

*Bobolinks with Black-eyed
Susans and Clover. Mixed media. 1973.*

*Baltimore (Northern) Orioles in Flowering
Dogwood. Mixed media. 1973.*

70

Ruby-throated Hummingbird Chasing a Hawk Moth. Mixed media.
(From a project for Life *magazine.) 1948.*

Swamp Rose-Mallow, Crimson-eyed Rose-Mallow, Wild Geranium, Pasture Rose,
Purple-Flowering Raspberry, Musk Mallow (clockwise from top left). From the 1968
Peterson Field Guide to Wildflowers of Eastern North America. 73

"What he taught me more than anything was the importance of observation. When you went out on a field trip with Peterson you took in every movement and sound; you saw things; you took an interest in what was around you. And this can apply to other things in life— the cultivation of an ability to make the most of a situation you're in."

— **Elliot Richardson**
Former Attorney General

A Field Guide to the Birds

INCLUDING ALL SPECIES FOUND
IN EASTERN NORTH AMERICA

A Bird Book on a New Plan

Roger Tory Peterson

THE FIELD GUIDES

Opposite: The topography of a bird, from the first edition of *A Field Guide to the Birds*. Peterson's use here of such words as *mandibles, scapulars,* and *axillaries* was a rare concession to academic terminology. His guides are rigorously written in everyday, conversational language. As always, his gift is to simplify, and never to talk down to readers. Previous page: Cover of the original, 1934 guide.

THE PUBLICATION OF PETERSON'S FIRST GUIDE IS STILL THE SINGLE MOST revolutionary development in American birding. The guide democratized birding, transferring it from the hands of a largely academic and museum-oriented elite. By converting birding into a mass activity of ordinary Americans, it helped to create the base for the environmental movement that started in the 1930s and burst forth more fully in the 1960s and 1970s.

Other guides had appeared before Peterson's. Some even featured color. But most were bulky, long-winded, and frustrating to use. Written by professional ornithologists working with dead specimens, they featured finicky, beak-to-tail descriptions that buried useful pointers in a confusing mass of detail.

Peterson cut through all that. His guides take the vantage point of the birder in the field who may have only a few seconds, often in poor light, to identify a bird. So the new "Peterson system," as it came to be called, was geared to instant impression and tell-tale field marks. It was based on Peterson's bold assumption that every bird has a distinctive fingerprint that can be explained succinctly in art and words.

Scaups were "black on both ends and white in the middle." The American Goldfinch is "the only small yellow bird with black wings." And Kirtland's Warbler can be picked out because "no other gray-backed warbler" wags its tail.

These lines were masterpieces of compression. Eight words told the story of the Screech Owl: "the only small eastern owl with ear tufts." Compression served another purpose: it kept the guide small enough to fit into a birder's pocket in the field. Peterson realized that fat guides are the ones birders leave at home.

In his field guide art, too, Peterson pared away all marginal detail. His schematic, two-dimensional paintings and drawings emphasized what birders needed to look for. Arrowlike lines jabbed toward the illustration, prodding the reader to notice the bird's two or three unique marks. Peterson put similar birds together in similar poses, usually on the same page. He taught readers to eliminate by deduction: if the glimpsed bird was one of three possible species, and

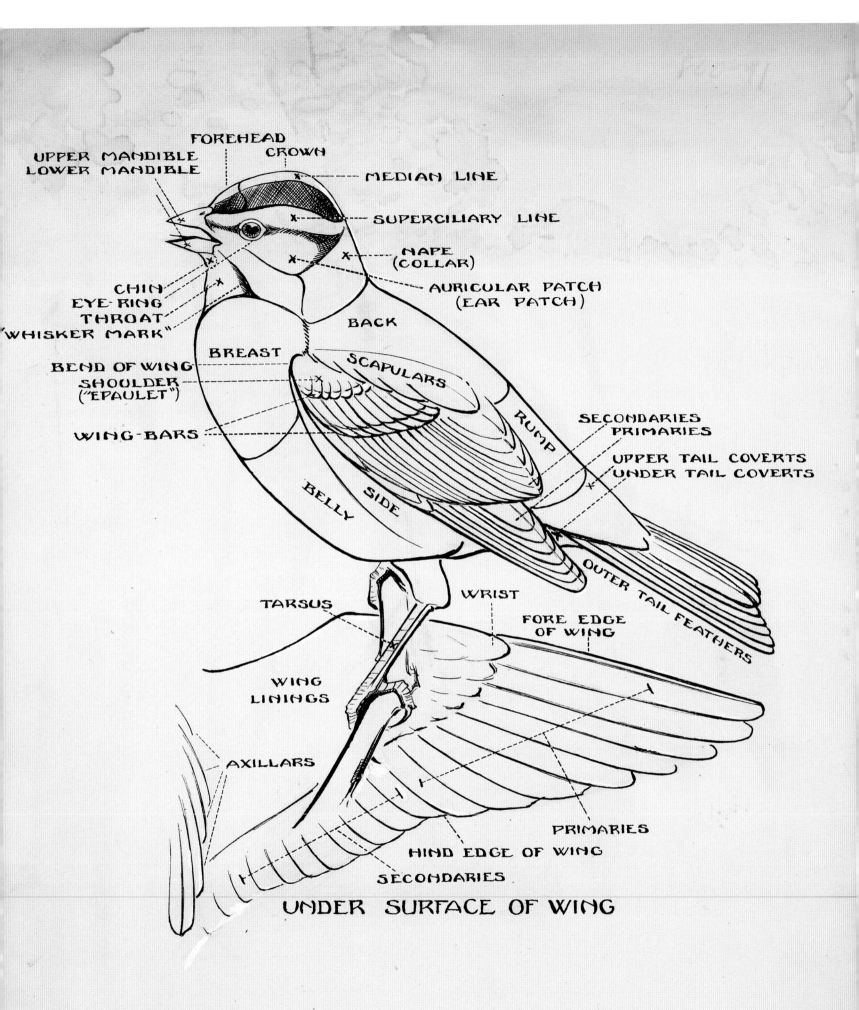

UPPER MANDIBLE
LOWER MANDIBLE

FOREHEAD
CROWN

MEDIAN LINE

SUPERCILIARY LINE

NAPE
(COLLAR)

AURICULAR PATCH
(EAR PATCH)

CHIN
EYE-RING
THROAT
"WHISKER MARK"

BACK

BREAST

SCAPULARS

BEND OF WING
SHOULDER
("EPAULET")

RUMP

SECONDARIES
PRIMARIES

UPPER TAIL COVERTS
UNDER TAIL COVERTS

WING-BARS

BELLY

SIDE

OUTER TAIL FEATHERS

TARSUS

WRIST

FORE EDGE
OF WING

WING
LININGS

AXILLARS

PRIMARIES

HIND EDGE OF WING

SECONDARIES

UNDER SURFACE OF WING

field marks could eliminate two, then the birder could identify the correct species even in cases where the bird was not well sighted.

Peterson has sold more than seven million copies of his bird guides, including one for Western North America, one for Texas (commissioned by the state's fish and wildlife commission) and two foreign guides done with collaborators: Britain and Europe and Mexico. Remarkably, he did all the illustrations as well as text for the North American guides himself. By contrast, the impressive National Geographic guide of the 1980s was the work of sixteen artists and thirty writers.

Like most revolutions, the Peterson revolution seems obvious in retrospect. By 1934 the era of shotgun birding was drawing to a close. Binoculars

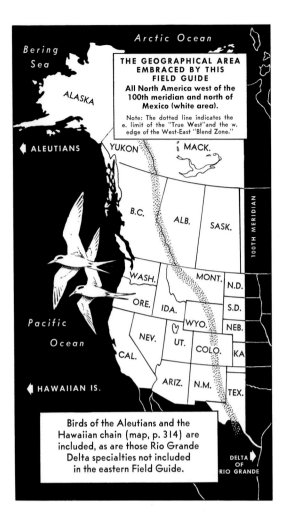

Peterson's illustrations are the work of a born teacher. Maps are instantly clear and informative. This map was reproduced in the field guide for Western North America and combines Virginia Marie Peterson's map with a Peterson illustration.

Silhouettes clearly show the body postures and varied leg positioning on American ducks. (The stiff-tailed ducks, second from right, have legs so far back for diving that they can hardly function on land.)

Above: The Cliff Swallow seen from above in flight and the flicker (above, with the trademark Peterson arrow) are shown with their distinct light rumps. Opposite page and left: The shorebird heads, woodpeckers in flight, and crested songbirds show Peterson's technique of grouping similar birds in similar poses for easier identification of distinguishing marks.

In the 1941 Western guide, Peterson packed 25 warblers (far left) and finches and finch-like birds (far right) onto a single plate. In the current version (1990), eight color pages cover 48 species of warblers, including rarities and

Stray Eastern Warbler (this page, left). Yellowish finches (this page, right) as shown in the most recently updated western guide. Though cramped for space and short on color illustrations, Peterson's early guides are still in demand: his text had not yet been shortened so that words and pictures could be positioned on opposite pages.

Constantly shifting bird populations can mean that a map is "out of date the day it is published," a common maxim in the bird world. Virginia Marie Peterson (opposite) makes the maps for the Peterson bird guides, an arduous and challenging task that requires constant checking with regional books and hundreds of correspondents. Nine years of work went into the 1,662 (breeding and winter) maps for 831 species in the recent Eastern and Western North American guides. Red depicts the summer range and blue shows the winter range of each species. The purple overlap indicates year-round range.

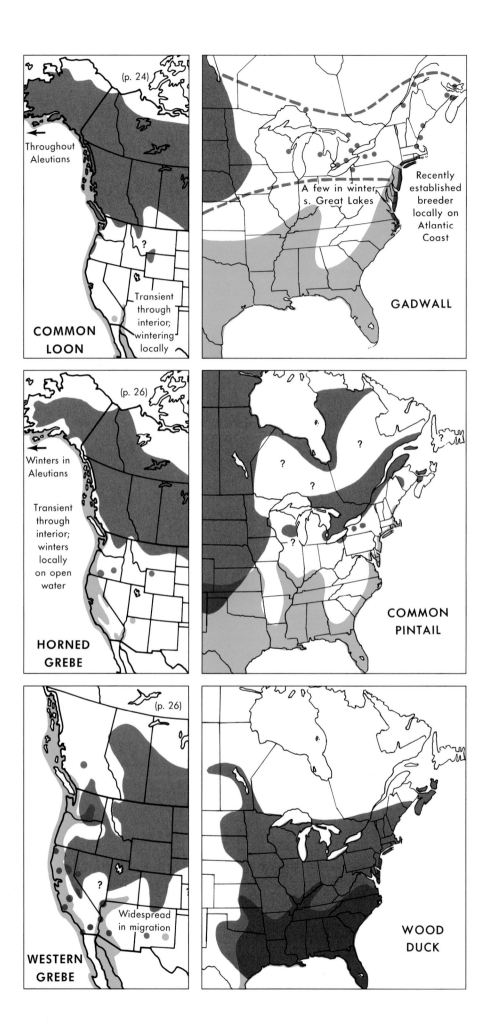

(p. 24)

Throughout Aleutians

Transient through interior; wintering locally

COMMON LOON

A few in winter, s. Great Lakes

Recently established breeder locally on Atlantic Coast

GADWALL

(p. 26)

Winters in Aleutians

Transient through interior; winters locally on open water

HORNED GREBE

COMMON PINTAIL

(p. 26)

Widespread in migration

WESTERN GREBE

WOOD DUCK

were improving. More and more birders were in the field, and they needed help. But the revolution required an extraordinary combination of talents: facility in language as well as art, a high ability to compress and edit, and the nonacademic background of an obsessive bird watcher with enormous confidence in his own field skills.

Among other things, Peterson erased the pessimism about bird identification that took hold during the shotgun era. Accustomed to examining the bird in hand, experts found it hard to believe that ordinary bird watchers could ever learn to tell certain species apart in the field. Before Peterson, one expert said flatly that female Common Mergansers and female Redbreasted Mergansers could not be told apart by sight in the wild. Now even beginning birders can distinguish them, even at some distance. That's one measure of the revolution. Peterson has taught two generations of field birders how to see.

In retrospect, Peterson has occasionally used the word "crude" to describe some of the early illustrations for his first guide. But the page of gulls (right) from the first Eastern guide is rendered with a lightness and simplicity of line that have strong aesthetic power. Opposite: Geese, shorebirds, and wading birds (all from the 1941 Western guide) and a page of small auks from the 1961 revised Western guide.

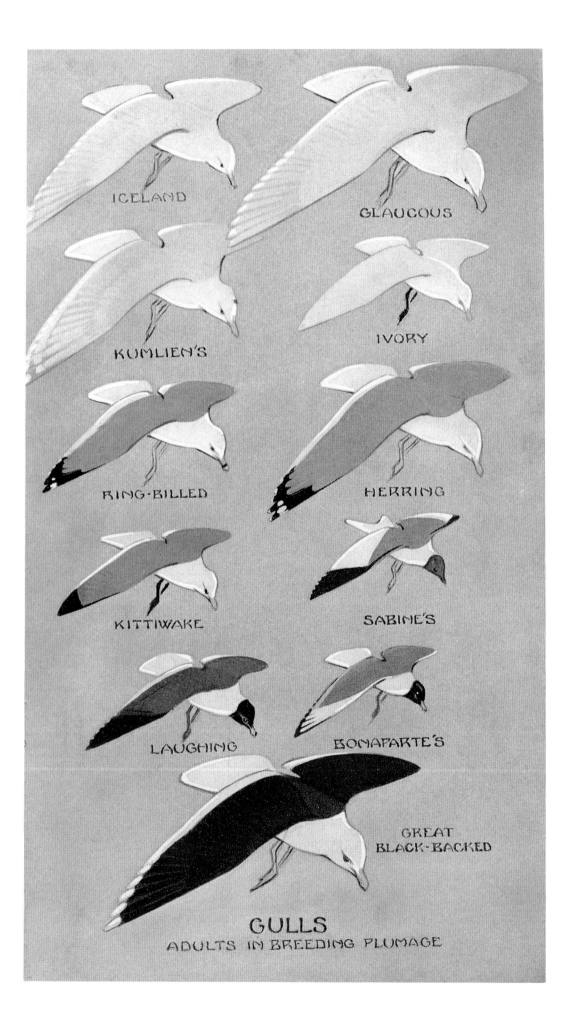

ICELAND

GLAUCOUS

KUMLIEN'S

IVORY

RING-BILLED

HERRING

KITTIWAKE

SABINE'S

LAUGHING

BONAPARTE'S

GREAT BLACK-BACKED

GULLS
ADULTS IN BREEDING PLUMAGE

CACKLING, LESSER CANADA and COMMON CANADA GEESE

SNOW GOOSE

ROSS'S GOOSE

WHITE-FRONTED GOOSE
ADULT   IMMATURE

BLACK BRANT

EMPEROR GOOSE

TRUMPETER SWAN   WHISTLING SWAN

BLACK-NECKED STILT

AVOCET

LONG-BILLED CURLEW

BLACK OYSTER-CATCHER

MARBLED GODWIT

SOLITARY SANDPIPER

WILLET

WANDERING TATTLER
FALL

RUDDY TURNSTONE
BREEDING

LESSER YELLOW-LEGS

SURF-BIRD

STILT SANDPIPER
FALL

ALEUTIAN SANDPIPER

BLACK TURNSTONE

WILSON'S PHALAROPE
FALL

SHOREBIRDS I

BLACK-CROWNED NIGHT HERON
ADULT   IMMATURE

AMERICAN BITTERN

LEAST BITTERN

YELLOW-CROWNED NIGHT HERON
ADULT

GREEN HERON
ADULT

IMMATURE   LITTLE BLUE HERON

LITTLE BLUE HERON   ADULT

GREAT BLUE HERON

SNOWY EGRET

HERONS

LOUISIANA HERON

AMERICAN EGRET

87

Ducks in flight from the 1994 Eastern guide (right) and in profile on the water from the 1980 Eastern guide (opposite). As usual, Peterson helpfully shows the most easily confused birds together: Canvasback with Redhead at top, Greater and Lesser Scaups, shown below with the similar Tufted Duck, a rare visitor.

On a single page, Peterson deftly compares a group of closely related terns in the 1980 Eastern guide (left). With similar economy, his 1961 Western guide deals with dark birds of prey seen from directly below, the most common vantage point of the birder (opposite).

A page of plovers from the 1990 Western guide (opposite), one of flycatchers (this page), including the dazzling Scissor-tailed Flycatcher, from the 1990 Western guide. Peterson once said four illustrations per page would be ideal. His pictures are now much larger, but the need to keep each guide pocket-sized often means more birds per page than is ideal.

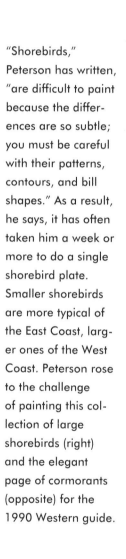

"Shorebirds," Peterson has written, "are difficult to paint because the differences are so subtle; you must be careful with their patterns, contours, and bill shapes." As a result, he says, it has often taken him a week or more to do a single shorebird plate. Smaller shorebirds are more typical of the East Coast, larger ones of the West Coast. Peterson rose to the challenge of painting this collection of large shorebirds (right) and the elegant page of cormorants (opposite) for the 1990 Western guide.

Icteridae: blackbirds and grackles (this page), Redwinged and Yellowheaded Blackbirds and Bobolink (opposite), both plates from the 1990 Western guide. Before Peterson, guides generally showed one illustration or photo for each species. Now most show male, female, and immature, often accompanied with other plumages and molts, reflecting the increased skill and interest of North American birders.

Brilliant pages of
tanagers (right), from
the 1990 Western
guide, and buntings
with Blue Grosbeak
(opposite) from the
1994 Eastern guide.

Toucans and a Scarlet Macaw (this page) and a page of parrots (opposite). Peterson found in Mexico some of his most brilliant subjects and avidly chose to paint 48 original plates for the 1973 *Field Guide to Mexican Birds*. "Noisy and gaudily colored" is Peterson's succinct description of Mexico's parrots. Some of these birds are now nesting in the United States. Though two native parrots, the Carolina Parakeet and the Thick-billed Parrot are extinct in the U.S., the Thick-billed has been reintroduced in Arizona, and a dozen parrot species, escaping from crates at Miami's International Airport, can be seen in Florida.

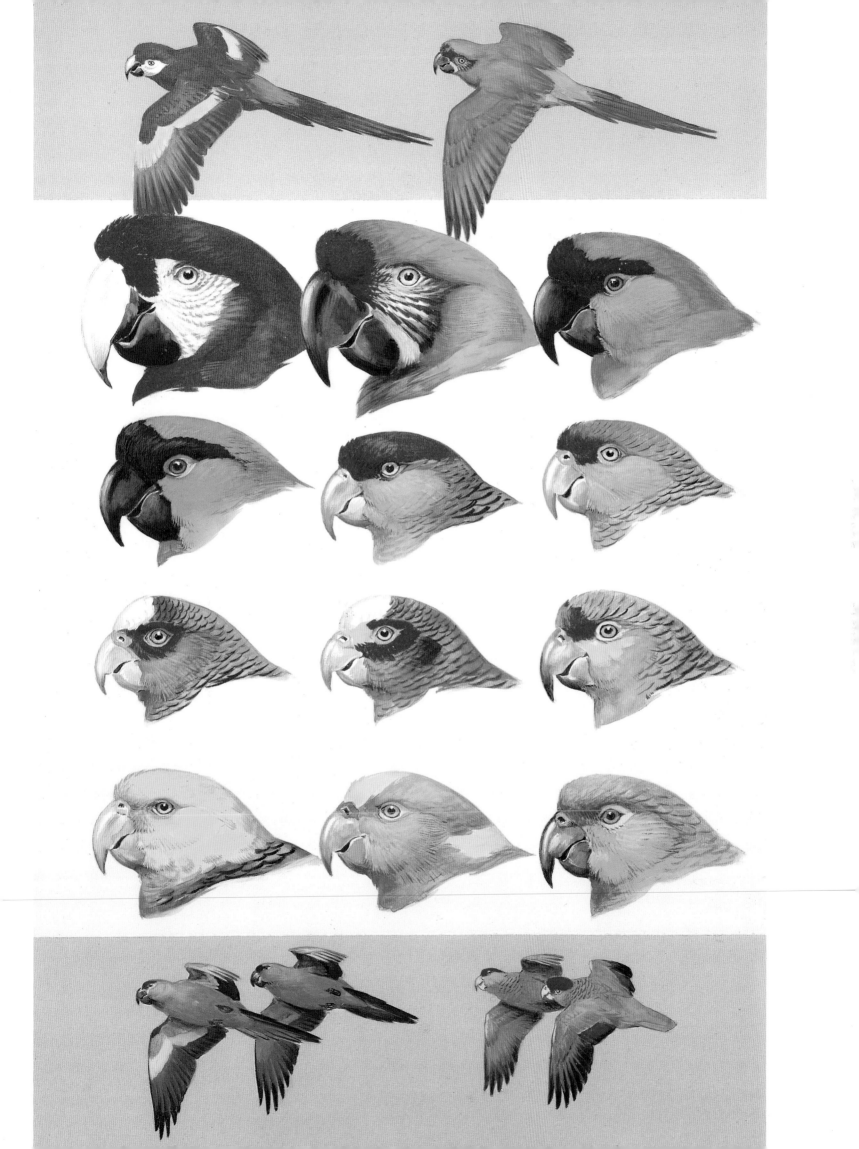

Owls (opposite) and a page of eagles and other large birds of prey (right), both from the Mexican guide. Some owls have two eyelike marks on the back of their heads, so that possible attackers from behind may think that they are being watched.

Hummingbirds from the Mexican guide. The dazzling iridescent colors come from laminations on feather surfaces. The brilliant flashing is used for sexual attraction and dominance display.

Woodpeckers *(Picidae)* are chisel-billed, long-tongued birds with spiny tails that brace them as they climb trees looking for insects, berries, and nuts (right). As shown on this page from the Mexican guide, some of the most colorful are found in Mexico, which boasts 25 species. Opposite: A splendid montage of cuckoos, anis, roadrunners, potoos and nightjars from the Mexican guide.

Crowded pages of jays and orioles from the Mexican guide. Though a smaller country, Mexico has far more bird species than the United States and Canada combined, so Peterson had to compress severely to keep the Mexican guide to a manageable pocket size.

Bustards (this page) are large long-legged striders of Europe's open plains, whereas the sandgrouse with which they sometimes associate are plump, dovelike birds of the desert. Opposite: In this carefully organized colorplate from his European guide, Peterson shows the smaller game birds—the grouse, ptarmigan, partridges, and quail.

The Wallcreeper of
Europe's mountains
(this page), like the
Hoopoe (opposite)
recalls a butterfly
when it flies from
cliff to cliff.
The Hoopoe, as
shown in the newest
European guide
(1993), has an erec-
tile crest and recalls
a butterfly in flight.

This page: The wag-tails of Europe are a real challenge to the birder. They are best sorted out by their head patterns.
Opposite: Wagtails are shown as they stand, in profile.
Both plates are from Peterson's European guide.
The arrows as shown here are used on nearly all plates and are a key part of the "Peterson System."

"I've always enjoyed photography because there's an immediacy to it. It's like hunting, but you're not taking life; you're recording life."

— Roger Tory Peterson

Photography

The Black Swan
of Australia has
become established
in New Zealand,
where these photo-
graphs were taken.
Posturing with curved
necks is a habit
shared by the white
Mute Swans of
Europe, which are
also found in North
America's parks.

White-faced Whistling Ducks in Venezuela. Whistling Ducks, a link between ducks and geese, are long-legged, long-necked birds with a some-what comic appear-ance. White-faced Whistling Ducks fly in large, dense flocks in Africa and South America. (They were formerly called Tree Ducks.)

Flightless
Cormorants, in the
Galápagos Islands.
Peterson writes of
the Galápagos:
"Nowhere else in the
world can one shoot
more film than in
these islands—easily
eight to ten rolls a
day, at point-blank
range—seldom
resorting to any lens
with a focal length
of more than 300
millimeters."

Previous pages:
Thirty species of
cormorants swarm
the seas of the
world, nesting
colonially on coastal
cliffs and islands.

Following page: A
pair of Double-
crested Cormorants
at attention in
Englewood, Florida.
Female in the fore-
ground, male behind.

Previous page: Willets at attention on a watery sandbar off the roadside dike at the Ding Darling Refuge in Florida.

Right: Tufted Puffin and Parakeet Auklets, Pribilof Islands, Alaska. They are both members of the Auk family, which replaces the penguins in northern oceans. The Pribilofs are a group of four islands in the Bering Sea, 285 miles off Alaska. The two largest, St. Paul and St. George, have spectacular seabird colonies, attracting birders from around the world.

Far right, top: Parakeet Auklets jawing, Pribilof Islands.
Middle: Crested Auklet and Least Auklets, Pribilof Islands.
Bottom: Snowy Owls sometimes nest in the Pribilofs not far from colonies of auks.

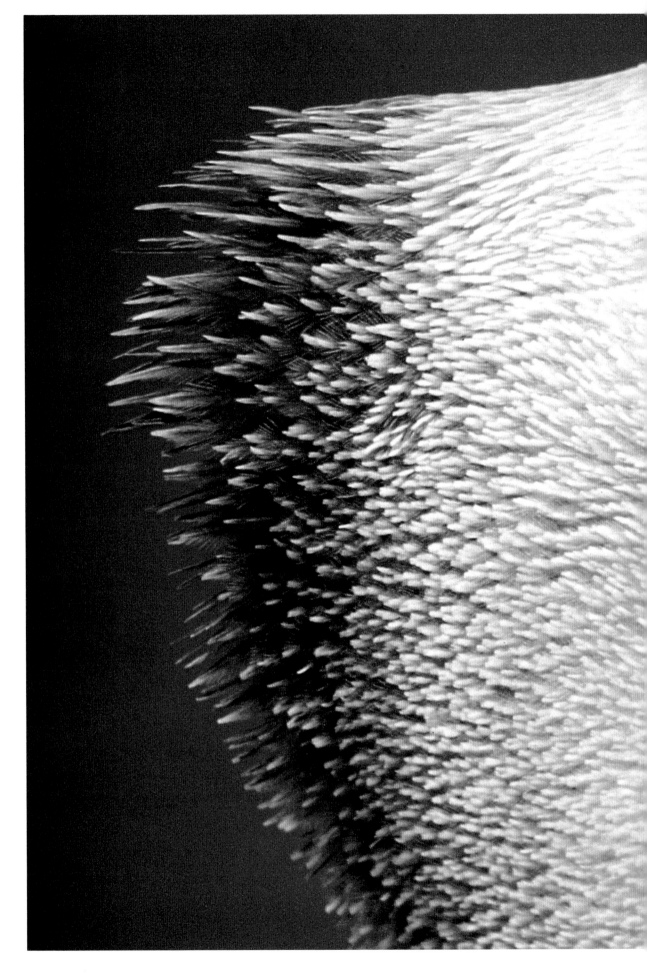

Right: An immature
Australian pelican,
Sydney, Australia.

Following pages:
Eurasion White
Pelicans (top left)
photographed in
1993 at Lake Nakuru
in Kenya. Peterson
was partly instru-
mental in persuading
the Kenyan govern-
ment to set aside
Nakuru as a wildlife
refuge. Brown peli-
cans (bottom left)
eagerly waiting to
be fed at a fish-
cleaning dock, near
Sanibel, Florida.
Right: A Wood Stork,
perhaps the most
homely bird in North
America, is numer-
ous in southern
Florida. It was for-
merly known as the
Wood Ibis.

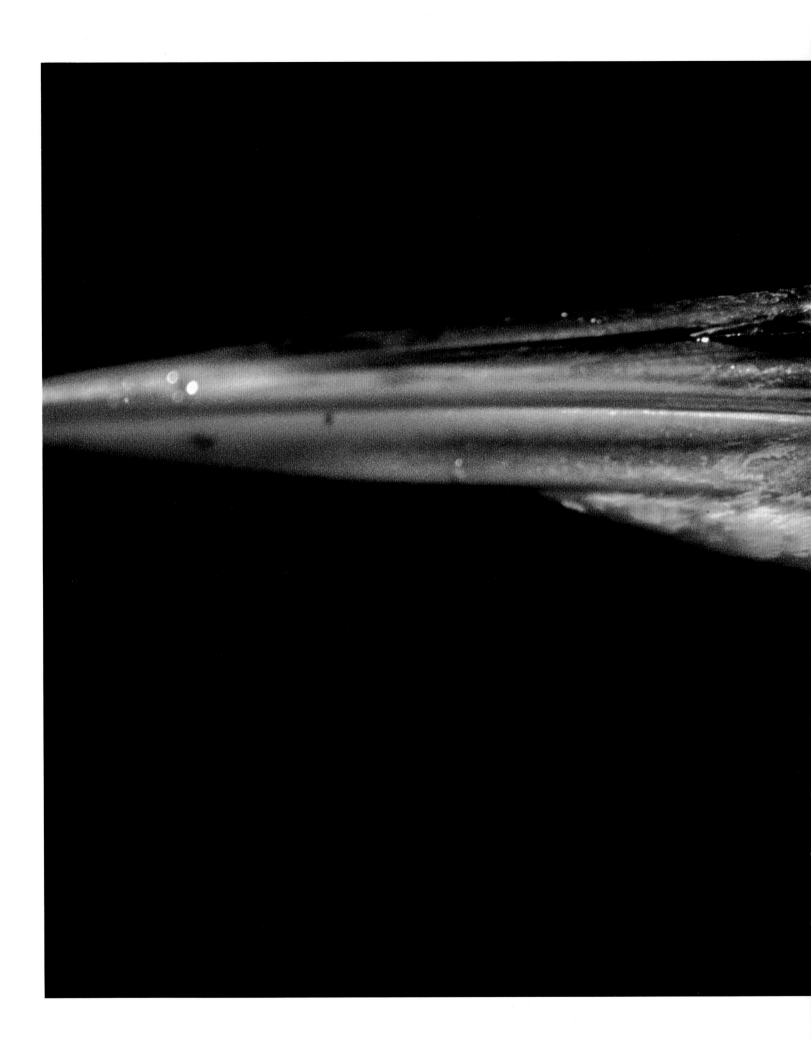

Previous pages:
Great Egret between
Fort Myers and
Sanibel Island,
Florida's Gulf Coast.
This bird, the largest
of America's egrets,
was formerly known
as the "Common
Egret" and the
"American Egret."
Today birders
refer to it as the
"Great Egret."

Right: Great Egret in
nuptial plumage,
Ding Darling Refuge,
Florida. America's
egrets and herons
were nearly wiped
out by plume hunters
and eggers at the
turn of the century.
The successful cam-
paign to save the
egrets gave birth to
the early environ-
mental movement.

Opposite, top: Great
Egret, between Fort
Myers and Sanibel
Island on Florida's
Gulf Coast.
Opposite, bottom:
Snowy Egret, Ding
Darling Refuge. Note
the bird's yellow
"slippers."

Little Blue Heron photographed at Tween-waters Inn, near Sanibel Island, Florida. This adult, at least five years old, depended on the fishermen at the inn for its daily meal of bait fish.

Above: "Crazy Egret" is the nickname for the Reddish Egret of the Gulf Coast, shown here in white and dark morphs. The birds move erratically while feeding in shallow water, alternating long, slow strides in a semi-crouched position while hopping and dancing about.

Right: A Roseate Spoonbill on the Texas coast, where many nest on the barrier islands.

Opposite: The Jabiru, a stork of tropical America, photographed in Brazil, is recognized by its massive bill and the red band across its swollen neck.

Left: A Green Kingfisher photographed from a small boat while drifting along the riverine woods in Venezuela.

A White Stork with
chicks on a nest in
Alsace, not far from
the Rhine River,
where the nests are
protected by
villagers. The storks
are often shot at for
target practice as
they migrate to the
Middle East. They
nest in trees and on
buildings, as well as
in marshes and
swamps.

Following pages:
Of the eighteen
kinds of storks in the
world, the Painted
Stork of India is one
of the most striking.

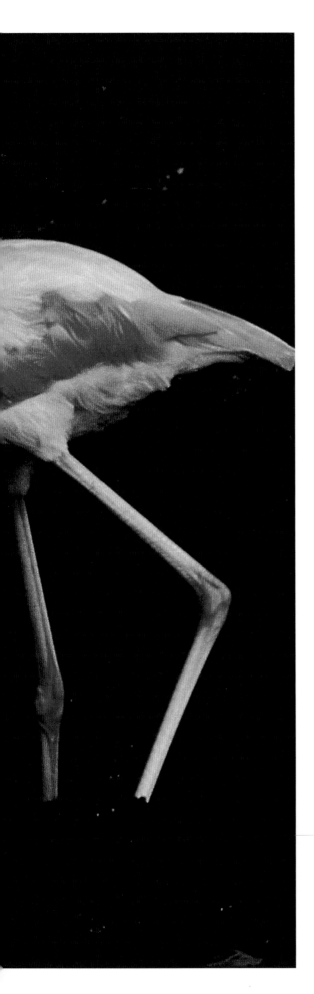

Above: Lesser
Flamingos congre-
gate by the hundreds
of thousands on the
saline flats of Lake
Nakuru in the
Rift Valley of Kenya,
where they are
rigidly protected.
Left: Greater
Flamingos photo-
graphed near their
colony at Andros
Island in the
Bahamas.

Right: Of the half-dozen kinds of flamingos in the world, only the West Indian race of the Greater Flamingo is bright pink throughout. This bird was photographed at close range from a blind at Andros Island in the Bahamas.

Left: Ospreys on a nest, Old Lyme, Connecticut. Large and graceful fish-eating birds, the species declined disastrously after the introduction of DDT, but the birds have made a spectacular comeback since DDT has been banned.

Following pages: Bald Eagles, Klamath, Oregon. "I am not an obsessed lister," Peterson writes. "An obsessed bird photographer, perhaps. I would rather shoot a roll of film on some relatively well-known species than add a new bird to my life list. Well, almost."

The Griffon Vulture,
top, and at right
eating the remains of
a wildebeest, is one
of the world's
heaviest flying birds.
This macabre scene
was photographed
in the Mara at the
border of Kenya and
Tanzania, where
the herd animals are
concentrated.

Opposite: A White-crested Turaco. This banded captive was photographed in western Kenya.

Top left: Cape Sugarbird on a Flowering Protea in a park near Cape Town. Note the long, wispy tail and curved bill.

Bottom left: Hildebrandts Starling at the edge of a bird bath near Nairobi in Kenya. There are more than 100 kinds of starlings in the Old World, most of them more beautiful than our introduced Eurasion Starling.

This page, top:
King Vulture at
a zoo in Brazil; and
Crowned Pigeon,
New Guinea.
Bottom: Yellow-
Knobbed Curassow,
Venezuela; and
Ross's Turaco,
western Kenya.

Opposite page, top:
Sulphur-crested
Cockatoo, Australia;
and Caracara at the
Pantanal, Brazil.
Bottom: Crowned
Crane, Kenya; and
Vulturine Guinea-
Fowl, Kenya.

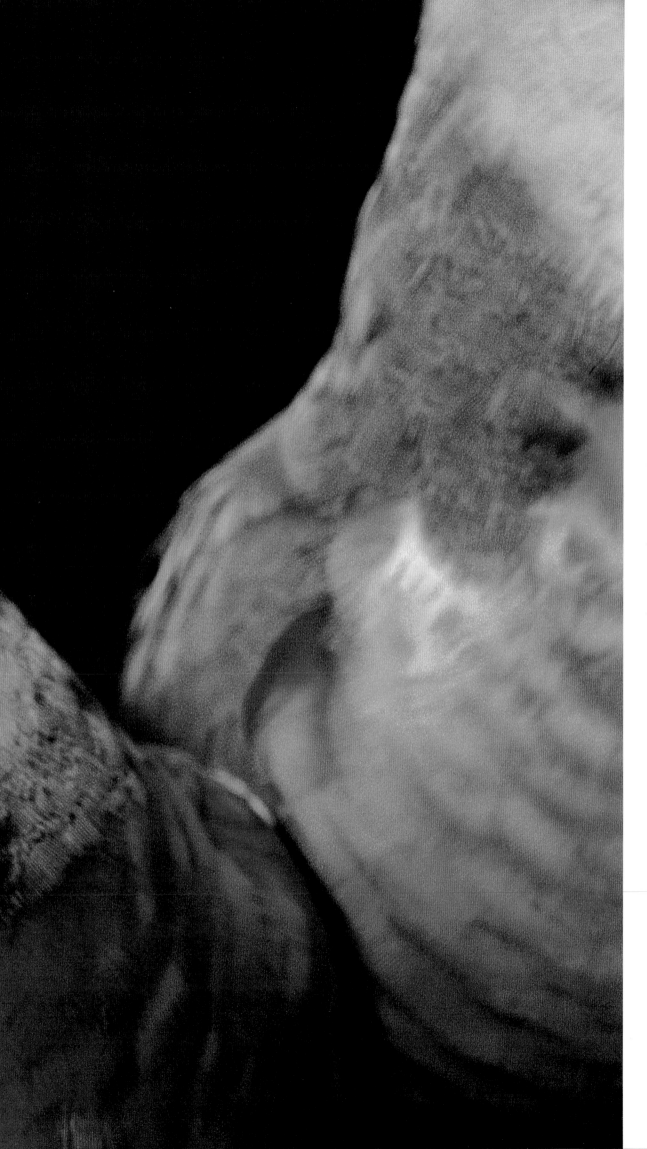

Rainbow Lorikeet at Corrumbin in Queensland, eastern Australia, where thousands of this bird are attracted to people's homes by trays of bread dipped in honey.

Following pages: A male Peacock displaying on a rajah's estate in India. No other bird can match the beauty of a male Peacock in full display.

Opposite: Hartlaub's
Gull, a South African
specialty photo-
graphed at a dock in
Cape Town.
Left: Silver Gull,
a small beauty
photographed off
Australia's east coast.

Royal Terns on the Chandeleur Islands, Gulf Coast of Louisiana. The Chandeleurs, off the delta of the Mississippi River, were formed when the river changed course and cut a new channel. On the islands, which are teeming with terns, the minimum distance between crowded birds is determined by the length of a jabbing beak.

Above: The Antarctic
Tern, like many other
terns, has a black
cap but is dustier
beneath, contrasting
with its white cheeks.
Right: Black
Skimmers on a sandy
island off the coast
of Texas.

Above: Albatross,
South Georgia.
Right: Cape Petrels
fly alongside a ship
off South Georgia,
in the South Atlantic.
Peterson says the
tube-noses—the
albatrosses, shear-
waters, petrels, and
storm-petrels—are
"the true mariners,
living their entire
lives at sea and
coming ashore on
remote islands to
nest and feed their
young."

Cape Gannets north of Cape Town, South Africa. Huge concentrations of birds are more readily photographed, not painted, Peterson says. "Too much is going on in a bird colony to sit and sketch."

Albatrosses are large birds with considerable wingspans that thrive in the open ocean, particularly in the Southern Hemisphere. In an almost textbook demonstration, this albatross shows off the dramatic banking turn that characterizes its gliding ability.

Adélie Penguins,
Hope Bay on the
Antarctic Peninsula.
The world has 17
species of penguins,
all in the Southern
Hemisphere, but not
all in the Antarctic.
The cold Humboldt
Current allows some
of them to move
north. Six species
live in temperate
seas, one species
even reaching to
the Equator.

Following pages:
Royal Penguins com-
ing down the narrow
trail from their
rookery, a half mile
into the hills of
Macquarie Island,
south of New
Zealand, the only
place in the world
where they breed. At
Nuggets's Point, on
the broad, black
beach as many as
100,000 gather to
loaf and to socialize
among the blubbery
masses of elephant
seals.

Opposite: The Rockhopper, the most widespread penguin, breeds by the millions on both sides of the Southern Hemisphere. In the Falklands, Peterson writes, "Tens of thousands of the beguiling doll-like birds swarm over the rocky slopes that drop jaggedly to the sea."

Left: Emperor Penguins on the ice near McMurdo. Emperors breed only on floating ice and seldom come to land. These huge birds, some weighing more than ninety pounds, seem "too ponderous, too ante-diluvian to belong to today's world," Peterson writes.

Magellenic Penguins off the coast of Patagonia, Argentina. Penguins are flightless, long-lived, and usually faithful for life to their mates. Their coloration—black on the back, white on the front—follows that of most seabirds. It allows swimming penguins to blend into their environment, looking light like the sky from below, dark like the sea from above.

Magellenic Penguins, shown here in the Falkland Islands, are sometimes known as "jackass" penguins because of their donkeylike bray. Peterson writes, "The mooing, bleating and cackling outside my tent sounded like a demon's barnyard. From the newly dug burrows around me came not only heart-rending, woeful cries but also the most loving of sounds."

Previous pages and right: Gatherings of King Penguins in the Bay of Isles, South Georgia. The ship offshore is the *Lindblad Explorer,* which pioneered Antarctic tourism, introducing thousands of humans to these droll birds that stand erect, like little people.

"The sort of thing I remember most about Roger Tory Peterson is this: In mid-conversation about mundane matters at the busy headquarters of the Audubon Society in the middle of New York City (not far from the reservoir in Central Park), Roger would pause, hearing the call of a bird, and say: 'Ah, that's a laughing gull.'"

— **Amy Clampitt**
Writer

Born August 28, 1908, in Jamestown, New York

1920 At age eleven he first becomes interested in nature after joining a Junior Audubon Club; he begins drawing birds. A year later he develops a passion for butterflies and moths.

1922 He buys his first camera, a Primo no. 9 4x5" plate camera, and shortly after switches back from pursuing butterflies to studying birds. He buys a bird guide by Chester Reed and a four-power Le Maire opera glass from an advertisement in *Bird Lore.*

1923 He begins keeping lists and daily logs of notes on birds. (He now estimates that in his lifetime he has seen nearly five thousand of the world's nine thousand species.)

1925 At age sixteen he graduates from Jamestown High School with distinction in design and mechani-

Above: Roger Tory Peterson with his mother, Henrietta Bader, 1908.

cal drawing. Just after his seventeenth birthday he is employed by the Union-National Furniture Factory in Jamestown to decorate Chinese-lacquer cabinets under the supervision of Willem Dieperink von Langereis. He publishes his first article in *Bird Lore.* He attends his first annual convention of the American Ornithologists' Union (A.O.U.) in New York City in November and submits two of his first watercolors to its exhibition of

> *"Birds pose readily for Roger Tory Peterson, as well they should. He is their greatest champion."*
> — Downs Matthews

bird art. He meets Ludlow Griscom, pioneer of field identification using field glasses, and Louis Agassiz Fuertes, the renowned bird painter, whose work has influenced him.

1926–1927 He attends the Art Students League in New York City; studies under distinguished teacher Kimon Nikolaides (author of *The Natural Way to Draw*) and leading painter John Sloan. He takes classes in basic drawing and life drawing from models (using charcoal and later oil on canvas).

1928–1931 He competes for and receives a place at the National

Academy of Design, where he studies under Raymond Neilson, Vincent DuMond, and Edmund Dickinson. He draws and paints from models.

He attends bimonthly meetings of the Linnaean Society in New York, where he meets members of the Bronx County Bird Club (which he joins), nine young men who teach him the tricks of identifying birds in the field, making it possible for him to consolidate information and give it artistic form in his first field guide, published in 1934.

During this period he acts as counselor of nature study at a YMCA camp in Michigan (one summer) and then at Camp Chewonki in Maine (five summers).

1931–1934 He teaches art and natural history at River's School, a private school for boys in Brookline, Massachusetts (now in Weston). Pupils in his classes include Elliot Richardson, later Attorney General of the United States. (In 1974 Richardson nominates Peterson as the teacher who influenced him most. Subsequently Peterson is named "Teacher of the Year" and given the Golden Key Award from the American Association of School Administrators.)

In 1932 he publishes three articles on duck identification in *Field and Stream,* using schematic illustrations that presage his first field guide.

In 1933 he presents the first significant exhibition of his bird paintings (four canvases in oil) at the annual convention of the American Ornithologists' Union in New York.

In April 1934 *A Field Guide to the Birds* is published by Houghton Mifflin in Boston after Peterson is introduced to the publisher by John B. May, state ornithologist of Massachusetts. The editors are Francis H. Allen, Paul Brooks, and, later, Austin Olney and Harry Foster. The first edition, which covers the birds of North America east of the Great Plains, includes 425 species with over 500 drawings in color and black-and-white by Peterson. The system of identification is visual rather than phylogenetic: similar-looking birds are assembled schematically on pages and key field marks or characteristics are identified with arrows. The first printing of two thousand copies sells out within three weeks, and the book is immediately reprinted. There have since been four revised and expanded revisions. A reported forty-seven printings and more than seven million copies of Peterson's two North American field guides to birds (East and West) have been sold.

1934–1943 He is elected a full member of the American Ornithologists' Union in 1935; a fellow in 1948; and later becomes vice-president.

He joins the staff of the National Association of Audubon Societies in 1934 as educational director. Acts as art director of *Bird Lore* (now *Audubon* magazine); he

Roger Tory Peterson, in his early twenties, with a 4x5" Auto-Graflex camera.

Peterson with a lacquered cabinet at the Union-National Furniture Factory, Jamestown, New York.

illustrates most of the covers at first, and from 1935 to 1950 writes the column "Bird's Eye View." The educational leaflets he writes on birds and illustrates with marginalia build the yearly membership of the Junior Audubon Clubs from 100,000 annually to 400,000. Later (1960 to 1964) he becomes secretary of the National Audubon Society and continues as a special consultant.

He becomes associated with

the stamp program of the National Wildlife Federation beginning in 1938 (with fourteen songbird paintings), first as artist, then as art director, and later as consultant. He is still active with the federation in choosing and arranging the annual collection of thirty-six commissioned art works that are published as stamps to raise funds for wildlife conservation and the purchase of wetlands.

Peterson photographing birds in 1942, near the Washington, D.C., airport.

Peterson on a boat trip in Maine in the early 1930s.

Peterson setting up a blind in Maine in the early 1930s.

Peterson filming with his first movie camera in Maine.

In 1938 he begins a series of color stories for *Life,* using his paintings, photography, and writing to present a broad spectrum of bird studies for a national audience.

In 1938 he revises the requirements for the Boy Scouts' Bird Study Merit Badge and prepares the official booklet about the badge.

1940–1943 Although he has volunteered earlier to work with pigeons as message carriers, he is drafted into the United States Army Corps of Engineers at Fort Belvoir, where he becomes first sergeant. His original assignment is in designing camouflage, but he is reassigned to producing instruction manuals because of his background with field guides.

His field guide principles are used by artists and writers under the supervision of Joseph Kastner of *Life* magazine to prepare a "plane-spotting manual" for that magazine, which will be used later by the Air Corps as a basis for a training manual for plane identification. Later he is transferred to the Air Corps in Orlando to help pioneer research on the effects of DDT on wildlife.

He befriends Rachel Carson during this period. They are fellow

Above: Preliminary cover for *Life* magazine by Peterson.

Middle top: Cover for *Bird Lore* (now *Audubon* magazine) by Peterson.

Middle bottom: Stamp of Snow Geese by Peterson for National Wildlife Federation.

Peterson in the field in the 1960s.

directors of the District of Columbia Audubon Society. Carson's work at the Fish and Wildlife Service has been preceded by Peterson's DDT work at Orlando. She has learned her birds from his field guide.

1944 He receives the William Brewster Memorial Award, the highest honor of the American Ornithologists' Union, for his contributions to ornithology.

1947 The Peterson Identification System is extended by Houghton Mifflin to cover other nature subjects. The Peterson Field Guide Series, of which Peterson is the editor, now embraces more than fifty titles (not including the

Peterson First Guides, which are for beginners).

1950 He receives his first literary award for nature writing, the John Burroughs Medal.

Gus Munzer begins printing large lithographs of his paintings for Quaker State.

He befriends James Fisher, Britain's best-known ornithologist; they travel together to Gotland Island in the Baltic and then to Finland. They are to co-author books and articles. Via Fisher he meets and works with Prince Philip, Lord Alanbrook, Sir Julian Huxley, Sir Peter Scott, Keith Shackleton, Eric Hosking, and other leading English birders. Peterson and Scott later help to

pioneer the World Wildlife Fund.

1952 He receives an honorary Doctor of Science degree from Franklin and Marshall College, the first of twenty-two honorary doctorates he will receive. (See page 204.)

1953 He makes a transcontinental tour of North America with James Fisher that will result in the book, *Wild America,* published by Houghton Mifflin in 1955.

A film, *Wild America,* made in 1953, will be shown in Russia in 1957. It is the first film on American wildlife to be shown in the U.S.S.R.

1954 He authors and illustrates

Virginia and Roger Tory Peterson on expedition in the Antarctic (seated on a whale's skeleton).

A Field Guide to the Birds of Britain and Europe with Guy Mountfort and Phil Hollom.

He receives his first major international award: the Geoffrey St. Hilaire Gold Medal from the French Natural History Society.

1960s He participates in international bird protection conferences in Tokyo, Cambridge, and Amsterdam and in scientific expeditions to Patagonia in 1960 (Yale), Galápagos in 1964, and Antarctica in 1965.

1961 He receives the Gold Medal of the New York Zoological Society.

1968 He first joins Lindblad Travel on an expedition to Antarctica. From then on travels with Lars-Eric Lindblad are to be a perennial part of Peterson's life, including seventeen trips to Antarctica, two to Tristan da Cunha (the most remote inhabited island in the Atlantic), and excursions to the Arctic, Europe, Asia, South America, and Africa (including the Okavango in Botswana and the Serengeti). He will be instrumental in the creation of a national park at Lake Nakuru in Kenya.

1970s He begins an active campaign to prevent DDT spraying in Connecticut.

He begins an active effort to bring the osprey back to New England. Approximately 150 known pairs within a radius of 10 miles from Old Lyme had declined to fewer than 10 pairs by the 1970s because of the DDT syndrome. (They have since made a comeback.)

He becomes honorary president of the International Committee for Bird Protection (ICBP).

1971 He receives the Conservation Medal of the National Audubon Society.

1972 He receives the Gold Medal of the World Wildlife Fund from Prince Bernhard of the Netherlands in the presence of Prince Juan Carlos (now King of Spain). He is the first American to receive this award.

1973 He receives the Joseph Wood Krutch Medal from the Humane Society of the United States. He begins a series of limited edition lithographs from his paintings for Mill Pond Press, printed under the supervision of Bob Lewin.

1974 He receives the Explorers Medal from the Explorers Club. A retrospective exhibition of his paintings is held at the American Museum of Natural History in New York City.

1975 He gives the keynote address to the Earth Care Conference of the United Nations.

1976 He receives from King Carl XVI of Sweden the Linnaeus Gold Medal of the Royal Swedish Academy of Sciences and is named "Swedish American of the Year." He begins with Virginia Marie Peterson an exhaustive study of bird distribution in North America for maps in the revised field guide to Eastern North America (390 maps done in three years) and the revised field guide to Western North America (440 maps done in six years).

1978 He is awarded the Order of the Golden Ark by Prince Bernhard of the Netherlands.

1980 He receives from President Jimmy Carter the Presidential Medal of Freedom, the highest honor awarded to an American civilian. First recipient of Ludlow Griscom Award from American

Architect Robert A. M. Stern and Peterson at the opening of The Roger Tory Peterson Institute, Jamestown, New York, 1993.

The Roger Tory Peterson Institute, Jamestown, New York, 1993.

Virginia Marie Peterson in front of a Peterson mural of penguins.

Birding Association for excellence in field birding.

1983 He is nominated for the Nobel Peace Prize.

1984 On the occasion of the fiftieth anniversary of the first edition of *A Field Guide to the Birds,* the Smithsonian Institution in Washington, D.C., honors Peterson with a major retrospective exhibition of his art and a publication, *Roger Tory Peterson at the Smithsonian.* He also receives the James Smithson Bicentennial Medal from the Smithsonian Institution. He publishes the first of numerous articles for *Bird Watcher's Digest,* becoming a regular bimonthly columnist. The column is called "All Things Reconsidered."

1993 The Roger Tory Peterson Institute building is dedicated in Jamestown, New York; the building has been designed by American architect Robert A. M. Stern. The mission of the institute, launched several years earlier, is "to inform society about the natural world through the study and teaching of natural history." The current director is Paul Benke; its president is Arthur Klebanoff.

BIBLIOGRAPHY

Books authored or co-authored by Roger Tory Peterson

A Field Guide to the Birds (Eastern North America). Boston: Houghton Mifflin, 1934 (revised 1939, 1941, 1947, 1980, 1994).

The Junior Book of Birds. Boston: Houghton Mifflin, 1939.

A Field Guide to Western Birds. Boston: Houghton Mifflin, 1941 (revised 1961, 1990).

The Audubon Guide to Attracting Birds (with John H. Baker). National Audubon Society, 1941.

Birds over America. New York: Dodd, Mead & Company, 1948.

How to Know the Birds. Boston: Houghton Mifflin, 1949.

Wildlife in Color. Boston: Houghton Mifflin, 1951.

A Field Guide to the Birds of Britain and Europe (with Guy Mountfort and P.A.D. Hollom). London and Boston: Collins and Houghton Mifflin, 1953 (also in 14 European languages). Revised and enlarged in 1993.

Wild America (with James Fisher). Boston: Houghton Mifflin, 1955.

A Bird-Watcher's Anthology. New York: Harcourt Brace, 1957.

A Field Guide to the Birds of Texas and Adjacent States. Boston: Houghton Mifflin, 1960.

The Birds (with the editors of *Life*). New York: *Life* Nature Library, Time, Inc., 1963. (Young Readers' Edition, 1967).

The World of Birds (with James Fisher). New York: Doubleday, 1964.

A Field Guide to Wildflowers of Northeastern and North-central North America (with Margaret McKenny). Boston: Houghton Mifflin, 1968.

Save the Birds (with Antony W. Diamond, Rudolf L. Schreiber, Walter Cronkite). Boston: Houghton Mifflin, 1987.

A Field Guide to the Birds of Mexico (with Edward Chalif). Boston: Houghton Mifflin, 1973. Translated and enlarged in Spanish. Mexico City: Diana, 1989.

Penguins. Boston: Houghton Mifflin, 1979.

The Audubon Society Baby Elephant Folio (with Virginia Peterson). New York: Abbeville Press, 1981.

The Field Guide Art of Roger Tory Peterson (two large volumes). Norwalk, Connecticut: Easton Press, 1990.

Illustrator (in part or in whole)

The Hawks of North America, by John B. May. Washington, D.C.: National Association of Audubon Societies, 1935.

South Carolina Bird Life, by Alexander Sprunt. Columbia, S.C.: University of South Carolina, 1949.

Birds of Newfoundland, by Harold Seymour Peters. Boston: Houghton Mifflin, 1951.

Arizona and Its Bird Life, by Herbert Brandt. Cleveland, Ohio: The Bird Research Foundation, 1951.

Birds of Nova Scotia, by Robie W. Tufts. Halifax: Nova Scotia Museum, 1961.

Birds of Colorado, by Alfred M. Bailey and Robert J. Niedrach. Denver: Denver Museum of Natural History, 1965.

Birds of New York State, by John Bull. Garden City, New York: Doubleday, 1973.

Selected Forewords and Introductions (in addition to volumes in the Peterson Field Guide Series)

Passage to Anywhere, by Lars-Eric Lindblad, 1983.

Songbirds in Your Garden, by John K. Terres, 1986.

Tales of a Low-Rent Birder, by Pete Dunne and David Sibley, 1986.

The Bird Illustrated, by Joseph Kastner, 1989.

A Birder's Guide to Southern California, by Harold Holt, 1990.

Ocean Birds of the California Pacific, by Rich Stallcup, 1990.

The Traveling Birder, by Clive Goodwin, 1991.

California: Vanishing Habitats and Wildlife, by B. "Moose" Peterson, 1992.

Nature's Everyday Mysteries: A Field Guide to the World in Your Backyard, by Sy Montgomery, 1993.

So Cranes May Dance: A Rescue from the Brink of Extinction, by Barbara Katz, 1993.

Birds of Kenya and Northern Tanzania, by Dale Zimmerman, 1993.

Manual of Ornithology: Avian Structure and Function, by Noble Proctor and Patrick J. Lynch, 1993.

Birds of Massachusetts, by Richard R. Veit, Wayne Peterson, and Barry W. VanDusen, 1993.

Birding in Ohio, by Tom Thomson, 1993.

Ludlow Griscom: Ornithologist, Conservationist, and "Dean of the Birdwatchers," by William E. Davis, Jr., 1994.

HONORARY DEGREES

Doctor of Science, Franklin and Marshall College, 1952.

Doctor of Science, Ohio State University, 1962.

Doctor of Science, Fairfield University, 1967.

Doctor of Science, Allegheny College, 1967.

Doctor of Science, Wesleyan University, 1970.

Doctor of Science, Colby College, 1974.

Doctor of Humanities, Hamilton College, 1976.

Doctor of Humanities, Amherst College, 1977.

Doctor of Science, Gustavus Adolphus College, 1978.

Doctor of Humane Letters, Skidmore College, 1981.

Doctor of Fine Arts, University of Hartford, 1981.

Doctor of Letters, Bloomsburg University, 1985.

Doctor of Science, Connecticut College, 1985.

Doctor of Fine Arts, State University of New York, 1986.

Doctor of Fine Arts, Middlebury College, 1986.

Doctor of Humane Letters, Yale University, 1986.

Doctor of Arts, Long Island University, 1987.

Doctor of Science, University of Connecticut, 1987.

Doctor of Science, Memorial University of Newfoundland, 1987.

Doctor of Arts, MacMurray College, 1989.

Doctor of Science, Bates College, 1991.

Doctor of Humane Letters, Southern Connecticut State University, 1991.